**TEACHER'S PET PUBLICATIONS**

LITPLAN TEACHER PACK
for
Call It Courage
based on the book by
Armstrong Sperry

Written by
Barbara M. Linde, MA Ed.

© 2006 Teacher's Pet Publications
All Rights Reserved

The Lit Plan for *Call It Courage* has been brought to you
by Teacher's Pet Publications, Inc.

Copyright Teacher's Pet Publications 2006
All Rights Reserved
11504 Hammock Point
Berlin, MD 21811

Only the student materials in this unit plan may be reproduced.
Pages such as worksheets and study guides may be reproduced for use in the purchaser's classroom.

For any additional copyright questions, contact Teacher's Pet Publications.

www.tpet.com

TABLE OF CONTENTS *Call It Courage*

About the Author	5
Introduction	7
Unit Objectives	11
Reading Assignment Sheet	12
Unit Outline	13
Study Questions	17
Quiz/Study Questions (Multiple Choice)	24
Pre-Reading Vocabulary Worksheets	35
Lesson One (Introductory Lesson)	49
Nonfiction Assignment Sheet	53
Oral Reading Evaluation Form	55
Writing Assignment 1	59
Writing Evaluation Form	60
Writing Assignment 2	67
Extra Writing Assignments/ Discussion Questions	69
Quotations	71
Writing Assignment 3	74
Vocabulary Review Activities	75
Unit Review Activities	77
Projects	82
Unit Tests	85
Unit Resource Materials	123
Vocabulary Resource Materials	145

A FEW NOTES ABOUT THE AUTHOR
Armstrong Sperry

SPERRY, Armstrong (1897-1976) Armstrong Sperry was born on November 7, 1897 in New Haven, Connecticut. As a boy, he liked to draw pictures and write stories. His great-grandfather, Sereno Armstrong, was a sea captain, and the young Sperry was fascinated with his tales of Bora Bora in the South Seas Islands. Sperry attended the Yale Art School and then joined the Navy and served in World War I. After his tour of duty ended, he enrolled at the Art Students League in New York City.

Remembering his grandfather's tales, and a book by Frederick O'Brien called *White Shadows in the South Seas*, Sperry finally traveled on a sailing schooner from Tahiti to Bora Bora in June 1941. He lived on Bora Bora for several months, and used the information he learned about the island and its Polynesian inhabitants as background for several books, including *Call It Courage*.

Sperry returned from Bora Bora and lived in Connecticut with his wife and children. He wrote and illustrated many children's books, and also illustrated book for other authors. In September 1924 he again traveled to the South Pacific, returning home in June 1925. Sperry also took an automobile trip over the old Santa Fe Trail and later wrote books set in the American Southwest.

In 1940 Sperry won the Newbery Award for *Call It Courage*, which was his ninth book for children. Armstrong Sperry died in April 1976.

Many of Sperry's books are now out of print, but titles may be found at used or antique bookstores. The following is a partial listing of his works.
- *One Day with Manu*, Philadelphia, Winston, 1933.
- *One Day with Jambi in Sumatra*, Philadelphia, 1934.
- *Wagons Westward: The Old Trail to Santa Fe*. Philadelphia, 1935.
- *Call It Courage*. New York, Macmillan, 1942.
- *Thunder Country*. New York, Macmillan, 1952.

INTRODUCTION *Call It Courage*

This unit has been designed to develop students' reading, writing, thinking, listening, and speaking skills through exercises and activities related to *Call It Courage* by Armstrong Sperry. It includes twenty lessons, supported by extra resource materials.

The **introductory lesson** introduces students to *Call It Courage*. Following the introductory activity, students are given an explanation of how the activity relates to the book they are about to read. Following the transition, students are given the materials they will be using during the unit. They are also introduced to the nonfiction assignment. At the end of the lesson, students begin the pre-reading work for the first reading assignment.

The **reading assignments** are approximately 20 pages each; some are a little shorter while others are a little longer. Students have approximately 15 minutes of pre-reading work to do prior to each reading assignment. This pre-reading work involves reviewing the study questions for the assignment and doing some vocabulary work for 8 to 10 vocabulary words they will encounter in their reading.

The **study guide questions** are fact-based questions; students can find the answers to these questions right in the text. These questions come in two formats: short answer or multiple choice. The best use of these materials is probably to use the short answer version of the questions as study guides for students (since answers will be more complete), and to use the multiple-choice version for occasional quizzes. It might be a good idea to make transparencies of your answer keys for the overhead projector.

The **vocabulary work** is intended to enrich students' vocabularies as well as to aid in the students' understanding of the book. Prior to each reading assignment, students will complete a two-part worksheet for approximately 8 to 10 vocabulary words in the upcoming reading assignment. Part I focuses on students' use of general knowledge and contextual clues by giving the sentence in which the word appears in the text. Students are then to write down what they think the words mean based on the words' usage. Part II gives students dictionary definitions of the words and has them match the words to the correct definitions based on the words' contextual usage. Students should then have an understanding of the words when they meet them in the text.

After each reading assignment, students will go back and formulate answers for the study guide questions. Discussion of these questions serves as a review of the most important events and ideas presented in the reading assignments.

After students complete extra discussion questions, there is a vocabulary review lesson which pulls together all of the separate vocabulary lists for the reading assignments and gives students a review of all of the words they have studied.

Introduction, *Call It Courage*

Following the reading of the book, a lesson is devoted to the extra discussion questions/writing assignments. These questions focus on interpretation, critical analysis and personal response, employing a variety of thinking skills and adding to the students' understanding of the novel. These questions are done as a **group activity**.

Using the information they have acquired so far through individual work and class discussions, students get together to further examine the text and to brainstorm ideas relating to the themes of the novel.

The group activity is followed by a **reports and discussion** session in which the groups share their ideas about the book with the entire class; thus, the entire class gets exposed to many different ideas regarding the themes and events of the book.

There are **three writing assignments** in this unit, each with the purpose of informing, persuading, or having students express personal opinions. The first assignment is to **express personal opinions**. Students are asked to imagine that they are one of the young people who know Mafatu. They give their opinion about courage and fear and whether or not Mafatu is a coward. The second writing assignment is to **persuade**. Students are asked to take the role of a tribal member and persuade the others to find a way to help Mafatu overcome his fear. The third writing assignment is to **inform.** Students write from Mafatu's point of view and create a survival manual to share with the members of his tribe and those on the other islands.

In addition, there is a **nonfiction reading assignment**. Students are required to read a piece of nonfiction related in some way to *Call It Courage*. After reading their nonfiction pieces, students will fill out a worksheet on which they answer questions regarding facts, interpretation, criticism, and personal opinions. During one class period, students make oral presentations about the nonfiction pieces they have read. This not only exposes all students to a wealth of information; it also gives students the opportunity to practice public speaking.

The **review lesson** pulls together all of the aspects of the unit. The teacher is given four or five choices of activities or games to use which all serve the same basic function of reviewing all of the information presented in the unit.

A **project** is included for students to complete in groups after they have finished with the rest of the unit. This project will encourage students to use analysis and synthesis skills. It will also provide the teacher with a means of informal assessment.

The **unit test** comes in two formats: all multiple choice matching true/false or with a mixture of matching, short answer, and composition. As a convenience, two different tests for each format have been included.

Introduction, *Call It Courage*

There are additional **support materials** included with this unit. The **resource materials sections** include suggestions for an in-class library, crossword and word search puzzles related to the novel, and extra vocabulary worksheets. There is a list of **bulletin board ideas** which gives the teacher suggestions for bulletin boards to go along with this unit. In addition, there is a list of extra class activities the teacher could choose from to enhance the unit or as a substitution for an exercise the teacher might feel is inappropriate for his/her class. Answer keys are located directly after the reproducible student materials throughout the unit.

UNIT PLAN ADAPTATIONS – *Call It Courage*

Block Schedule
Depending on the length of your class periods, and the frequency with which the class meets, you may wish to choose one of the following options:
- Complete two of the daily lessons in one class period.
- Have students complete all reading and writing activities in class.
- Assign all reading to be completed out of class, and concentrate on the worksheets and discussions in class.
- Assign the projects from the daily lessons at the beginning of the unit, and allow time each day for students to work on them.
- Use some of the Unit and Vocabulary Resource activities during every class.

Gifted & Talented / Advanced Classes
- Emphasize the projects and the extra discussion questions.
- Have students complete all of the writing activities.
- Assign the reading to be completed out of class and focus on the discussions in class.
- Encourage students to develop their own questions.

ESL/ELD
- Assign a partner to help the student read the text aloud.
- Tape record the text and have the student listen and follow along in the text.
- Give the student the study guide worksheets to use as they read.
- Provide pictures and demonstrations to explain difficult vocabulary words and concepts.
- Conduct guided reading lessons, asking students to stop frequently and explain what they have read.
- Show the movie version of the novel (if available) and help students identify characters and events, and relate the action in their own words. You may want to show the movie without the sound and explain the actions in your own words.

UNIT OBJECTIVES – *Call It Courage*

1. Through reading *Call It Courage* students will analyze characters and their situations to better understand the themes of the novel.

2. Students will be introduced to the elements of a folktale or tribal legend.

3. Students will demonstrate their understanding of the text on four levels: factual, interpretive, critical, and personal.

4. Students will practice reading aloud and silently to improve their skills in each area.

5. Students will enrich their vocabularies and improve their understanding of the novel through the vocabulary lessons prepared for use in conjunction with it.

6. Students will answer questions to demonstrate their knowledge and understanding of the main events and characters in *Call It Courage*.

7. Students will practice writing through a variety of writing assignments.

8. The writing assignments in this are geared to several purposes:
    a. To check the students' reading comprehension
    b. To make students think about the ideas presented by the novel
    c. To make students put those ideas into perspective
    d. To encourage critical and logical thinking
    e. To provide the opportunity to practice good grammar and improve students' use of the English language.

9. Students will read aloud, report, and participate in large and small group discussions to improve their public speaking and personal interaction skills.

10. Students will complete a group project to further their understanding of *Call It Courage*.

READING ASSIGNMENT SHEET
Call It Courage

Date Assigned	Reading Assignment	Completion Date
	Chapter 1	
	Chapter 2	
	Chapter 3	
	Chapter 4	
	Chapter 5	

WRITING ASSIGNMENT LOG *Call It Courage*

Date Assigned	Writing Assignment	Completion Date
	Writing Assignment 1	
	Writing Assignment 2	
	Writing Assignment 3	
	Non-fiction Assignment	
	Project	

UNIT OUTLINE *Call It Courage*

1 Introduction	2 PVR Chapter 1 Nonfiction Assignment	3 Study ?? Chapter 1 PVR Chapter 2 Oral Reading Evaluation	4 Study ?? Chapter 2 Minilesson: Conflict	5 Writing Assignment #1
6 PVR Study ?? Chapter 3	7 Study?? Chapter 3 Writing Conference	8 Quiz Chapters 1-3 PVR Chapter 4	9 Study ?? Chapter 4 Minilesson: Character Traits	10 Writing Assignment #2
11 PVR Study?? Chapter 5	12 Extra Writing/ Discussion Questions	13 Writing Assignment #3	14 Vocabulary Review	15 Unit Review
16 Test	17 Nonfiction Assignment	18 Project	19 Project	20 Project

Key: P = Preview Study Questions   V=Vocabulary Work   R= Read

STUDY GUIDE QUESTIONS

SHORT ANSWER STUDY GUIDE QUESTIONS
Call It Courage

Chapter 1
1. What is the setting of the story? Include the time, the place, and the name of the group of people.
2. Who is the main character of the story? Include the character's age and his christened name. Include the character's new name, what the name means, and the character's relationship to the leader of the group.
3. What does the main character fear and why?
4. Why is the character's fear such a problem?
5. How do the older people treat the main character? What do they believe was at fault for the character's problem?
6. Who are the main character's two most constant companions?
7. One night the main character overhears Kana, one of the other boys, make a comment. What is the comment, how does the main character feel about it, and what does the main character do in response?

Chapter 2
1. What are the *Ara Moana*?
2. What happens to Mafatu and his canoe during the storm?
3. Describe the land that Mafatu sees in the distance.
4. How does Mafatu reach land?
5. What does Mafatu hear when he reaches the sand?
6. What does Mafatu do when he reaches land?
7. What happens to Uri?

Chapter 3
1. Describe Mafatu's physical condition when he wakes up on the island.
2. Which god does Mafatu think has carried him safely across the water?
3. What island did Mafatu originally think he was headed to? What does he realize when he looks around?
4. How does Mafatu tend to the wound on his leg?
5. What vow does Mafatu make, and to whom does he make it?
6. What does Mafatu discover when he looks at the banana trees? What does this discovery mean to him?
7. What does Mafatu discover at the end of the trail? What does he do when he arrives at the end of the trail?
8. How does Mafatu feel about his actions? Why does he feel that way?
9. What survival-related actions does Mafatu take next?
10. What thoughts does Mafatu have as he prepares to go to sleep?

Short Answer Study Guide Questions *Call It Courage*

Chapter 4
1. What does Mafatu discover about the tasks he did in Hikueru?
2. How does Mafatu begin to get the tamanu tree ready to use for a canoe?
3. What does Mafatu make while the canoe is building and why?
4. What does Mafatu use to make a new *pareu* to wear? Why is it important for him to have this article of clothing?
5. What does Mafatu use to make his tools? What tools does he make?
6. Describe how and why Mafatu kills the hammerhead shark. Include how Mafatu feels.
7. Describe how Mafatu kills the wild boar. Include how he feels about this accomplishment and what he does afterwards.
8. Describe what happens to Mafatu's knife while he is out fishing. Include what he does with the knife.
9. What does Mafatu do when he gets back to the island?
10. What sound wakes Mafatu?

Chapter 5
1. What does Mafatu see when he climbs to the top of the plateau?
2. What does Mafatu do when the men go after him?
3. Describe the chase.
4. Describe the rest of Mafatu's journey.
5. Describe Mafatu's homecoming.

ANSWER KEY: SHORT ANSWER STUDY GUIDE QUESTIONS
Call It Courage

<u>Chapter 1</u>

1. What is the setting of the story? Include the time, the place, and the name of the group of people.
    The story is set many years ago in the South Sea Islands. The people are Polynesians who live on the island/atoll of Hikueru.

2. Who is the main character of the story? Include the character's age and his christened name. Include the character's new name, what the name means, and the character's relationship to the leader of the group.
    The main character is a 15-year-old boy named Mafatu. He was originally christened "Stout Heart." His newer name means "The Boy Who Was Afraid." He is the son of Tavana Nui, the Great Chief of Hikueru.

3. What does the main character fear and why?
    Mafatu is afraid of the sea. When he was three, there was a great hurricane. Mafatu was out in a reef pool in a canoe with his mother. The canoe was carried out to sea. The canoe capsized and the two were carried to a small island. The mother saved the boy but she died.

4. Why is the character's fear such a problem?
    Mafatu belongs to a group of fishermen and is also the son of the leader. The others think Mafatu is useless and brings bad luck. They worry that Mafatu will not be able to provide food for himself or others. He may also not be able to lead the men in battle against the men of the other islands.

5. How do the older people treat the main character? What do they believe was at fault for the character's problem?
    The older people treat Mafatu well. They think the *tupapau,* or ghost-spirit that is in every child at birth is at fault for his fear.

6. Who are the main character's two most constant companions?
    They are Uri, a yellow dog and Kivi, an albatross with a deformed foot.

7. One night the main character overhears Kana, one of the other boys, make a comment. What is the comment, how does the main character feel about it, and what does the main character do in response?
    Kana is talking with the other boys. He says that they will all go out the next day to look for food—all except Mafatu, who is a coward. Mafatu feels resentment and decides he must prove his courage to himself and the group. He must go out and face Moana, the Sea God.

Answer Key Short Answer Study Guide Questions *Call It Courage*

Chapter 2
1. What are the *Ara Moana*?
    That is the ancient Polynesian name for the Paths of the Sea, or the ocean currents the Polynesian navigators used to travel the Pacific Ocean.

2. What happens to Mafatu and his canoe during the storm?
    A huge wave lifts the canoe and washes away all of Mafatu's possessions, including his clothing or *pareu*. The wave also destroys the canoe's sail and mast.

3. Describe the land that Mafatu sees in the distance.
    The land has a high mountain with trees growing from the shoreline.

4. How does Mafatu reach land?
    An ocean current carried the canoe over a barrier reef into the water near an island.

5. What does Mafatu hear when he reaches the sand?
    He hears the sound of fresh, running water.

6. What does Mafatu do when he reaches land?
    He drags himself to the edge of the jungle and collapses on the bank of the stream.

7. What happens to Uri?
    Uri survives and goes to the island with Mafatu.

Chapter 3
1. Describe Mafatu's physical condition when he wakes up on the island.
    He is thirsty and weak. His right leg is swollen and has a gash on the calf where he had cut it on some coral.

2. Which god does Mafatu think has carried him safely across the water?
    He thinks it was Maui, the God of the Fishermen.

3. What island did Mafatu originally think he was headed to? What does he realize when he looks around?
    He thought he was headed for Tahiti. When he looks around he realizes he is not on Tahiti.

4. How does Mafatu tend to the wound on his leg?
    He squeezes lime juice into the cut and wraps a bandage of *purau* leaves on it.

Answer Key Short Answer Study Guide Questions *Call It Courage*

5. What vow does Mafatu make, and to whom does he make it?
   Mafatu vows to Maui, the God of the Fishermen, that he will return to his father, Tavana Nui.

6. What does Mafatu discover when he looks at the banana trees? What does this discovery mean to him?
   He finds that the bananas have been cut off within the past week by knives. He thinks that he should find out who cut down the bananas.

7. What does Mafatu discover at the end of the trail? What does he do when he arrives at the end of the trail?
   He discovers a sacred place that belongs to the eaters-of-men. He also sees a spearhead, and, in spite of his fear, he takes the spearhead from the sacred platform.

8. How does Mafatu feel about his actions? Why does he feel that way?
   He is happy because he realizes that he succeeded in doing something that he was afraid of doing.

9. What survival-related actions does Mafatu take next?
   He makes a fire, cooks breadfruit and bananas for his and Uri's dinner, plaits some coconut fronds into screens, and chooses a tree to use for a canoe.

10. What thoughts does Mafatu have as he prepares to go to sleep?
    He is relaxed and happy. He has a new confidence and belief in himself because he has food, fire, and shelter. He successfully faced the Sea God. He took a spear from the sacred altar of the eaters-of-men and survived.

Chapter 4
1. What does Mafatu discover about the tasks he did in Hikueru?
   He finds out that the tasks, such as making nets and knives and fishhooks, are all things he needs to know now in order to survive. He is glad he has the skills to make the things he needs.

2. How does Mafatu get the tamanu tree ready to use for a canoe?
   First he built a fire at the base of the tree. After the fire had eaten into the trunk, Mafatu climbed the tree and jumped on a large branch. The tree fell over.

3. What does Mafatu make while the canoe is building and why?
   He builds a raft so that he can get out to the reef to set fish traps.

Answer Key Short Answer Study Guide Questions *Call It Courage*

4. What does Mafatu use to make a new *pareu* to wear? Why is it important for him to have this article of clothing?
    He uses the fibers of a mulberry tree to make the *pareu*. It is important for him to be well clothed when he returns home. He wants the others to realize that he has conquered the sea and land.

5. What does Mafatu use to make his tools? What tools does he make?
    He finds a whale skeleton and uses it to make a knife first. After that he makes an adze to use to carve out the canoe.

6. Describe how and why Mafatu kills the hammerhead shark. Include how Mafatu feels.
    Mafatu and Uri go out in the raft to set the fishing traps. Uri falls off the raft when a wave goes across the reef. The shark goes after Uri and Mafatu dives into the water. He is already angry at the shark for destroying the fish trap. Now is he in a rage because the shark is attacking his dog. Mafatu swims under the shark and stabs it in the belly. He kills the shark and Uri is unharmed. When he gets back to shore, Mafatu feels humble with gratitude. He realizes that he was able to kill the shark because of his feelings for the dog.

7. Describe how Mafatu kills the wild boar. Include how he feels about this accomplishment and what he does afterwards.
    Mafatu is climbing the trail to the top of the mountain when he hears noise in the underbrush. As the wild boar charges, Mafatu aims his spear. He kills the boar and makes a sled of bamboo to drag the dead animal down to his camp. There, he roasts the meat and makes a necklace of the tusks. When he puts on the necklace, he feels the magic of the boar making him strong.

8. Describe what happens to Mafatu's knife while he is out fishing. Include what he does with the knife.
    Mafatu is fishing in his new canoe when the knife falls overboard. He wants to get the knife, but it is deep down on the bottom of the sea and he has never dived that far. Also, he would have to dive past holes where the giant octopus might live. Mafatu decides to dive and gets his knife. On his swim back to the surface an octopus attacks him. He uses his knife to stab the octopus in both eyes, killing it. He keeps the body and plans to show the tentacles to the people at home.

9. What does Mafatu do when he gets back to the island?
    He prepares the canoe for his departure the next day. Then he goes to sleep.

10. What sound wakes Mafatu?
    The sound of drums wakes him. He realizes the drums belong to the eaters-of-men who are returning to the island.

Answer Key Short Answer Study Guide Questions *Call It Courage*

Chapter 5
1. What does Mafatu see when he climbs to the top of the plateau?
    He sees that the eaters-of-men are on the island and they are dancing at their sacred place. Then he sees four of the men running towards him.

2. What does Mafatu do when the men go after him?
    He runs to his canoe, gets in, and takes off.

3. Describe the chase.
    The eaters-of-men have six canoes that go after Mafatu. The wind is in his favor and he stays ahead. They chase him all day and into the night. Then the warriors begin falling behind. By dawn the next morning he does not hear or see them.

4. Describe the rest of Mafatu's journey.
    The winds hold for several days, then die down. Mafatu paddles on, and begins to see sharks. In frustration he shouts at Moana, the Sea God. Suddenly he sees a lagoon fire and realizes that Hikueru is just ahead of him. Kivi is in the air above him.

5. Describe Mafatu's homecoming.
    The people gather on the shore as the canoe comes in. No one recognizes Mafatu when he gets out and walks onto the beach. Then he greets his father. When his father realizes that this stranger is his son, he tells the people the boy's name is Stout Heart.

MULTIPLE CHOICE STUDY GUIDE/QUIZ QUESTIONS *Call It Courage*

<u>Chapter 1</u>
1. What is the setting of the story?
    A. The story is set in 1865 in Gettysburg, Pennsylvania.
    B. The story is set in Hawaii.
    C. The story is set in the Caribbean.
    D. The story is set many years ago in the South Sea Islands.

2. Who is the main character of the story?
    A. The main character is a 15-year-old boy named Mafatu.
    B. The main character is a 12-year-old boy named Kivi.
    C. The main character is a 10-year-old boy named Tavana Nui.
    D. The main character is a 16-year-old boy named Uri.

3. What does the main character fear and why?
    A. He is afraid of earthquakes because his father died in one.
    B. He is afraid of the village boys because they make fun of him.
    C. He is afraid of the sea because he and his mother were caught in a storm at sea when he was three.
    D. He is afraid of being away from his mother because she saved him when he almost drowned.

4. Why is the character's fear such a problem?
    A. Earthquakes frequently hit the island where he lives, so he lives in constant fear.
    B. He lives with an island tribe of fishermen and is the son of the leader. The people think he is useless, brings bad luck, will not be able to provide food, and will not be a good leader in battle.
    C. He won't leave his mother to go to school or to participate in activities with the other children in the village, and he is falling behind the other boys.
    D. He has to go to school with the boys, but his school work is suffering because he is so intimidated by them.

5. How do the older people treat the main character? What do they believe was at fault for the character's problem?
    A. They treat him with indifference. They think his problem is his own fault.
    B. They are kind to him because they think his father is to harsh with him.
    C. They treat him well. They think the ghost-spirit is to blame for his fear.
    D. They are nice to him. They feel sorry for him because the boys are so mean to him.

Multiple Choice Questions *Call It Courage*

6. Who are the main character's two most constant companions?
    A. They are Mafatu, the chief's son, and Stout Heart, his best friend.
    B. They are Uri, a yellow dog and Kivi, an albatross with a deformed foot.
    C. They are Tupapau and Hikueru, two other village boys.
    D. They are Tavana Nui, the chief, and Kana, a yellow dog.

7. One night the main character overhears one of the other boys make a comment. What is the comment, how does the main character feel about it, and what does the main character do in response?
    A. He says that Mafatu, is a coward. Mafatu feels resentment and decides he must prove his courage to himself and the group. He must go out and face Moana, the Sea God.
    B. He says that the chief, Mafatu's father, is very ill. Mafatu is deeply saddened and decides he must go offer himself as a sacrifice to Moana the Sea God.
    C. He says that Mafatu's mother has died at sea. He is overcome with grief and decides to take his canoe into the sea to try to find her.
    D. He says that Mafatu is a terrible fisherman, an embarrassment to the village. Mafatu decides to leave the village forever so his father, the chief, won't be embarrassed by him.

Multiple Choice Questions *Call It Courage*

Chapter 2
1. What are the *Ara Moana*?
	A. Paths of the Sea, or the ocean currents
	B. Lights of the Sky, or constellations
	C. Whispers of the Wind, or trade winds
	D. Arms of the Gods, or strong canoes

2. What happens to Mafatu and his canoe during the storm?
	A. The mast is struck by lightning, and Mafatu is left stranded.
	B. The waves toss the canoe side to side, and Mafatu gets seasick.
	C. The canoe breaks apart. Mafatu is forced to hold onto some floating debris, reminding him of when he almost drowned when he was three.
	D. A huge wave washes away all of his possessions including his clothing.

3. Describe the land that Mafatu sees in the distance.
	A. The land has a high mountain with trees growing from the shoreline.
	B. It appears to be glowing with beautiful colors.
	C. The land is a dry, sandy desert with no plants.
	D. The land is flat, just like his home, Hikueru.

4. How does Mafatu reach land?
	A. He paddles the canoe there.
	B. He ties a rope to Uri, who swims toward the shore with the boat in tow.
	C. An ocean current carries the canoe into the water near the island.
	D. Holding onto the floating debris and Uri, he kick-swims to the shore.

5. What does Mafatu hear when he reaches the sand?
	A. He hears his dog barking.
	B. He hears the sound of fresh, running water.
	C. He hears the wind blowing through the trees.
	D. He hears drums beating.

6. What does Mafatu do when he reaches land?
	A. He pulls himself into a small cave at the edge of the water.
	B. He rests against the trunk of a palm tree.
	C. He looks for food.
	D. He drags himself to the edge of the jungle and collapses on the bank of the stream.

7. What happens to Uri?
	A. Uri survives the canoe crash and is on the island with Mafatu.
	B. He is carried out to sea on a riptide.
	C. He protects Mafatu from the attack of a wild boar but is severely wounded.
	D. He drowns before he can swim to land.

Multiple Choice Questions *Call It Courage*

<u>Chapter 3</u>

1. Describe Mafatu's physical condition when he wakes up on the island.
    A. He is thirsty and weak. His right leg is swollen and has a gash on the calf.
    B. He has a broken leg but is otherwise fine.
    C. He is tired and hungry. His vision is blurred and his head hurts.
    D. He is weak and sore. He has swallowed too much sea water, but is okay.

2. Which god does Mafatu think has carried him safely across the water?
    A. He thinks it was Neptune, the Sea God.
    B. He thinks it was Maui, the God of the Fishermen.
    C. He thinks it was Poseidon, the Water God.
    D. He thinks it was Tuamotu, the God of Sailors.

3. What island did Mafatu originally think he was headed to?
    A. Bora-Bora
    B. Oahu
    C. Tahiti
    D. Papua New Guinea

4. How does Mafatu tend to the wound on his leg?
    A. He packs it with seaweed and wraps banana leaves around it.
    B. He makes a fresh cut to get it to bleed again, then he touches hot coals to it to cauterize it.
    C. He wraps it in *tupapau* leaves and prays to *Ara Moana.*
    D. He squeezes lime juice into the cut and wraps a bandage of *purau* leaves on it.

5. What vow does Mafatu make, and to whom does he make it?
    A. He makes a vow to Ara Moana to offer sacrifices to the gods every day.
    B. He makes a vow to Neptune to stay on the island for five years, to purge himself of his fear.
    C. He vows to his father that he will never return home.
    D. He vows to his mother that he will avenge her death.

6. What does Mafatu discover when he looks at the banana trees?
    A. He discovers monkeys live on the island.
    B. He sees that the bananas have been cut off with knives.
    C. He discovers that the bananas will not be ripe for weeks and wonders what he will eat.
    D. He can tell by the direction the trees are leaning that the prevailing winds are from the south.

Multiple Choice Questions *Call It Courage*

7. What does Mafatu discover at the end of the trail?
    A. He discovers a sacred place that belongs to the eaters-of-men.
    B. He discovers wild boar bones.
    C. He discovers an old dwelling.
    D. He discovers fresh water.

8. How does Mafatu feel about taking the spearhead? Why does he feel that way?
    A. He is happy because he realizes that he succeeded in doing something he was afraid of doing.
    B. He is afraid because he thinks the gods will be angry.
    C. He is unconcerned; it was there, he took it, and it was no big deal.
    D. He is proud to own such a fine weapon because the boys who made fun of him would be envious.

9. What survival-related actions does Mafatu take?
    A. He makes a signal fire and stores fresh water.
    B. He makes a fire, cooks breadfruit and bananas, plaits some coconut fronds into screens, and chooses a tree to use for a canoe.
    C. He builds a lookout-tower, makes a bamboo hut, and goes fishing.
    D. He shaves the ends of dried bamboo poles into points, forms bowls from coconuts to catch water, digs a pit to catch a wild boar, and make a fish trap.

10. What thoughts does Mafatu have as he prepares to go to sleep?
    A. He worries about the man-eaters.
    B. He wonders what his father and the boys are doing at the village.
    C. He wonders how he will ever survive on this island.
    D. He has a new confidence and belief in himself.

Multiple Choice Questions *Call It Courage*

Chapter 4

1. What does Mafatu discover about the tasks he did in Hikueru?
    A. He realizes just how useless his life has been to this point in time.
    B. He finds out that the tasks are all things he needs to know now in order to survive.
    C. He discovers how pampered he has been for all of his childhood.
    D. He thinks the tasks he did in Hikueru were "women's work," not suitable for helping a man survive in the world.

2. How does Mafatu begin to get the tamanu tree ready to use for a canoe?
    A. He builds a fire at the base of the tree.
    B. He makes a series of cuts at the base of the tree.
    C. He cuts off the largest branches of the tree.
    D. He digs around the roots of the tree.

3. What does Mafatu make while the canoe is building and why?
    A. He makes a bowl to hold the *mantua*, the waterproofing for the canoe.
    B. He constructs a bamboo boat ramp to launch the canoe.
    C. He makes a food safe to protect and store his food.
    D. He builds a raft so that he can get out to the reef to set fish traps.

4. Why is it important for Mafatu to have a new *pareu* to wear?
    A. Even though the island has lots of shade and trees, the sun is too strong for his skin. He needs protection from the elements.
    B. He wants to be well-clothed when he returns home so the others will realize that he has conquered the sea *and* the land.
    C. If the man-eaters come, it will give him some protection from their spears.
    D. The coral is sharp. When Mafatu goes diving the *pareu* will keep the sharp edges of the coral from cutting his skin.

5. What does Mafatu use to make his tools? What tools does he make?
    A. He uses rocks he finds inland to make a knife and a hammer.
    B. He uses the bones of a wild boar to make an adze and a spearhead.
    C. He uses pieces of coral and shells to make a knife, fish hooks, and needles.
    D. He uses a whale skeleton to make a knife and an adze.

Multiple Choice Questions *Call It Courage*

6. Describe how and why Mafatu kills the hammerhead shark.
    - A. The shark was stealing fish from his trap. Mafatu makes his spear into a harpoon and jabs it into the shark's head.
    - B. The shark was circling his new canoe. Afraid the shark would destroy it, Mafatu jumps overboard, waits for the shark to swim towards him, and stabs it in the eyes.
    - C. The shark was attacking his faithful and loving dog. In a rage, Mafatu dives into the water, swims under the shark, and stabs it in the belly.
    - D. Mafatu had dropped his knife in the water. When he dove into the water to get it, the shark attacked. Mafatu was just able to get his knife in time to kill it.

7. Describe how Mafatu feels about killing the wild boar.
    - A. He is proud and feels the magic of the boar-tooth necklace making him strong.
    - B. He is ashamed for killing the wild boar. He prays to Mona Loa to forgive him and wears the necklace of boar's teeth as a symbol of his shame.
    - C. He is sorry he had to kill the animal, but he needed the meat for food. He wears the boar-tooth necklace to remind himself of his own mortality.
    - D. He is glad he killed the boar because it had attacked Uri. He wears the necklace of boar's teeth as an outward sign of his successful revenge.

8. Describe what happens to Mafatu's knife while he is out fishing. Include what he does with the knife.
    - A. The knife is hanging from a string around his neck. The string breaks and the knife falls into the water. He wants to retrieve it but is too afraid to dive and get it. He leaves it there.
    - B. The knife falls overboard. Mafatu dives and gets his knife. On his swim back to the surface, an octopus attacks him, and he uses his knife to kill it.
    - C. The knife gets stuck in a fish that swims away. Mafatu tries to recover it, but his attempts are unsuccessful.
    - D. The knife falls into the water. Mafatu dives in after it, only to find that it has fallen into the mouth of a giant clam. He cannot retrieve it.

9. What does Mafatu do when he gets back to the island before he goes to sleep on what turns out to be his last night there?
    - A. He uses his knife to make a notch in the tree trunk to mark another day.
    - B. He goes to his lookout point to check for the man-eaters.
    - C. He prepares a big feast to celebrate his new-found courage and his good luck.
    - D. He prepares the canoe for his departure the next day. Then he goes to sleep.

10. What sound wakes Mafatu?
    - A. The sound of drums wakes him.
    - B. The sound of a canoe hitting the beach wakes him.
    - C. The sound of approaching footsteps wakes him.
    - D. The sound of a thunderstorm wakes him.

Multiple Choice Questions *Call It Courage*

Chapter 5

1. What does Mafatu see when he climbs to the top of the plateau?
    A. He sees a pack of wild dogs.
    B. He sees his dog, Uri.
    C. He sees that the eaters-of-men are on the island.
    D. He sees several canoes from Hikueru that have come to rescue him.

2. What does Mafatu do when the men run after him?
    A. He runs to his canoe, gets in, and takes off.
    B. He hides in the cave he found on the first day he arrived.
    C. He quickly tries to gather things he can trade with them.
    D. He's so glad to see people, he runs down to greet them.

3. Describe how the eaters-of-men chase Mafatu and tell the outcome.
    A. They chase Mafatu to the beach and give up when he sails away in his canoe.
    B. They go after Mafatu in their canoes. With the wind in his favor, Mafatu stays ahead. By dawn the next morning he does not hear or see them.
    C. They chase Mafatu for about an hour but then give up, since he would be such a small catch anyway.
    D. They are really only interested in getting back the spearhead Mafatu stole from the sacred place. Once they find it at Mafatu's camp, they only chase him a little further to make sure he doesn't take any more of their things.

4. Describe the last part of Mafatu's journey home.
    A. Mafatu sails right into the lagoon at Hikueru without any further problems.
    B. Mafatu recognizes the boats of many of the fisherman of Hikueru. He hails them, identifies himself, and follows them into the lagoon.
    C. Mafatu paddles on in his canoe and begins to see sharks. In frustration he shouts at Moana, the Sea God. Suddenly he sees a "lagoon fire" and realizes that Hikueru is just ahead of him. Kivi is in the air above him.
    D. Mafatu's canoe breaks apart on the reef at Hikueru. He holds onto the keel and paddles into Hikueru following Kivi.

5. Describe Mafatu's homecoming.
    A. Mafatu swims ashore. No one is there. When he goes to his father's house, his father welcomes him saying, "My son, forgive me."
    B. Mafatu's father was on one of the boats that came out to meet his canoe. When he sees Mafatu's fine canoe and the boar-tooth necklace, he declares that there will be a feast to honor Moana the Sea God for returning his son.
    C. It is ordinary. He goes home and continues making nets and hooks. Nothing changes.
    D. The people gather on the shore as the canoe comes in. No one recognizes Mafatu when he gets out and walks onto the beach. When his father realizes that this stranger is his son, he tells the people the boy's name is Stout Heart.

ANSWER SHEET MULTIPLE CHOICE STUDY GUIDE/QUIZ QUESTIONS
Call It Courage

Chapter 1	Chapter 2	Chapter 3
1. D	1. A	1. A
2. A	2. D	2. B
3. C	3. A	3. C
4. B	4. C	4. D
5. C	5. B	5. D
6. B	6. D	6. B
7. A	7. A	7. A
		8. A
		9. B
		10. D

Chapter 4	Chapter 5
1. B	1. C
2. A	2. A
3. D	3. B
4. B	4. C
5. D	5. D
6. C	
7. A	
8. B	
9. D	
10. A	

PREREADING VOCABULARY WORKSHEETS

Prereading Vocabulary Worksheets *Call It Courage*

Chapter 1

Part I: Using Prior Knowledge and Contextual Clues
Below are the sentences in which the vocabulary words appear in the text. Read the sentence. Use any clues you can find in the sentence combined with your prior knowledge, and write what you think the italicized word means in the space provided.

1. It happened many years ago, before the traders and *missionaries* first came into the South Seas. . . .

2. . . . while the Ploynesians were still great in numbers and *fierce* of heart.

3. So the people drove him forth. Not by violence, but by *indifference*.

4. Mafatu, the boy who had been christened *Stout* Heart by his proud father, was afraid of the sea.

5. The thunder of it filled his ears; the crash of it upon the reef, the *mutter* of it at sunset.

6. There were other canoes scattered at wide *intervals* along the reef.

7. It was the season of hurricane and the people of Hikueru were nervous and ill at ease, charged, it seemed, with an almost animal awareness of *impending* storm.

8. Mafatu would never forget the sound of his mother's *despairing* cry.

9. The woman sprang forward to *seize* her child as the canoe capsized.

10. The woman sprang forward to sieze her child as the canoe *capsized*.

11. When at last they were cast up on the *pinnacle* of coral, Mafatu's mother crawled ashore with scarcely enough strength left to pull her child beyond the reach of the sea's hungry fingers.

Prereading Vocabulary Worksheets *Call It Courage*

Chapter 1, continued

12. Mafatu's stepmother knew small sympathy for him, and his stepbrothers treated him with open *scorn*.

13. The boy stood there *taut* as a drawn arrow awaiting its release.

14. What matter if they *jeered*? For a second he almost turned back. Then he heard Kana's voice once more saying: "Mafatu is a coward."

Part II: Match the vocabulary words to their dictionary definitions.

_____ 1. missionaries   A. complain quietly or indistinctly
_____ 2. fierce   B. feeling hopeless
_____ 3. indifference   C. top; highest point
_____ 4. stout   D. mocked by shouting or laughing
_____ 5. mutter   E. brave, sturdy
_____ 6. intervals   F. people sent by a church to spread its faith
_____ 7. impending   G. stiff; stretched tight
_____ 8. despairing   H. caused a boat to overturn
_____ 9. seize   I. ferocious; violent
_____ 10. capsized   J. about to happen
_____ 11. pinnacle   K. contempt; disrespect
_____ 12. scorn   L. lack of interest or concern
_____ 13. taut   M. distances between things
_____ 14. jeered   N. take hold of quickly and firmly

Prereading Vocabulary Worksheets *Call It Courage*

Chapter 2
Part I: Using Prior Knowledge and Contextual Clues
Below are the sentences in which the vocabulary words appear in the text. Read the sentence. Use any clues you can find in the sentence combined with your prior knowledge, and write what you think the italicized word means in the space provided.

1. Day broke over a gray and *dismal* world.

2. The boy shuddered. His fingers gripped the paddle *convulsively*.

3. What skill had *wrought* this small canoe!

4. Then with a *rending* groan the mast cracked.

5. The boy lost all sense of time's passage. Every nerve became dulled by *tumult.*

6. Many the boy had seen, but this was a giant–a monster *livid* and hungry.

7. Uri crept toward the *prostrate* boy, quailing beside him, whimpering softly.

8. Uri crept toward the prostrate boy, *quailing* beside him, whimpering softly.

9. Now the air was *luminous* with promise of another day.

10. Out of the *sultry* mists the sea emerged, blue and violent.

11. A soft land breeze, heavy with a scent of flowers, wafted out across the dark waters, *tantalizing*, bitter-sweet.

12. Somewhere ahead a strip of beach, salt-white in the darkness, *lured* him onward.

Prereading Vocabulary Worksheets *Call It Courage*

Chapter 2, continued

Part II: Match the vocabulary words to their dictionary definitions.

_____ 1. dismal   A. in a violently jerking or shaking manner
_____ 2. convulsively   B. very angry
_____ 3. wrought   C. tempted
_____ 4. rending   D. giving off or reflecting light
_____ 5. tumult   E. tearing apart violently
_____ 6. livid   F. trembling or shrink back with fear
_____ 7. prostrate   G. depressing
_____ 8. quailing   H. tempting but unavailable
_____ 9. luminous   I. very hot and damp
_____ 10. sultry   J. lie flat
_____ 11. tantalizing   K. formed; created
_____ 12. lured   L. noisy uproar

Prereading Vocabulary Worksheets *Call It Courage*

Chapter 3
Part I: Using Prior Knowledge and Contextual Clues
Below are the sentences in which the vocabulary words appear in the text. Read the sentence. Use any clues you can find in the sentence combined with your prior knowledge, and write what you think the italicized word means in the space provided.

1. He sighed, and sank back on the mossy bank, *relishing* the strength that quickened his tired body.

2. Were they even now watching him from secret places in the jungle, biding their time? He glanced about in *apprehension.*

3. It was the cone of a long extinct volcano. From its base ridges of *congealed* lava flowed down to the distant shore.

4. His leg still pained, and he would need the juice of limes to *cauterize* the coral wound, and purau leaves to make a healing bandage.

5. From that point of *vantage* he would be able to survey his entire island and the sea for a distance of many miles.

6. In each case the opening was caused by a river which flowed from the mountain down into the lagoon; for the tiny coral polyp which builds its *ramparts* from the floor of the sea cannot withstand fresh water.

7. "I will burn it out, then make an *adze* of basalt to finish it."

8. The boy stood there *irresolute* and uncertain.

9. Some premonition of danger kept him *poised*, alert, and wary.

10. . . . on top of this pyramid a *grotesque* idol, hideously ugly, reared in the brilliant sunshine.

Prereading Vocabulary Worksheets *Call It Courage*

<u>Chapter 3, continued</u>

11. Weary with the *exertion*, Mafatu settled back on his haunches and watched the leaping flame.

12. Before long, perhaps. . . . Mafatu was certain of it, as he was certain that the sun shone and was warm. It was *inevitable*.

Part II: Match the vocabulary words to their dictionary definitions.

_____	1. relishing	A. bizarre; gross
_____	2. apprehension	B. physical effort that requires great strength
_____	3. congealed	C. a position that gives an advantage
_____	4. cauterize	D. became thick and solid
_____	5. vantage	E. impossible to prevent from happening
_____	6. ramparts	F. a tool for cutting heavy pieces of wood
_____	7. adze	G. worry; nervousness
_____	8. irresolute	H. balanced; suspended
_____	9. poised	I. taking great pleasure in
_____	10. grotesque	J. unsure; not able to make decisions
_____	11. exertion	K. walls of a fort
_____	12. inevitable	L. seal a wound with something that burns

Prereading Vocabulary Worksheets *Call It Courage*

Chapter 4
Part I: Using Prior Knowledge and Contextual Clues
Below are the sentences in which the vocabulary words appear in the text. Read the sentence. Use any clues you can find in the sentence combined with your prior knowledge, and write what you think the italicized word means in the space provided.

1. Mafatu could *fell* his tree by the fire, and burn it out, too.

2. It was a *veritable* treasure trove.

3. And thus they returned to the camp site, weary, but filled with *elation*.

4. Some sea robber had been breaking into his bamboo trap and he was going to find out who the *culprit* was!

5. "Aiá, Ma'o!" the boy shouted roughly, trying to *bolster* up his courage.

6. Mafatu was filled with *impotent* rage.

7. The boy made a *rude* sled of bamboo and loaded the heavy animal onto it.

8. There was something gloomy and *oppressive* in this high island.

9. With *dismay* the boy watched it descend.

10. Then darkness clouded the water as the octopus *siphoned* out his venom.

Prereading Vocabulary Worksheets *Call It Courage*

Chapter 4, continued
Part II: Match the vocabulary words to their dictionary definitions.

	_____ 1. fell		A. without strength to be helpful
	_____ 2. veritable		B. transferred liquid through a tube
	_____ 3. elation		C. cut down
	_____ 4. culprit		D. someone who is responsible for a misdeed
	_____ 5. bolster		E. a feeling of hopelessness or disappointment
	_____ 6. impotent		F. harsh
	_____ 7. rude		G. real; true
	_____ 8. oppressive		H. strengthen by encouraging
	_____ 9. dismay		I. a feeling of extraordinary happiness and excitement
	_____ 10. siphoned		J. rough; incomplete

Prereading Vocabulary Worksheets *Call It Courage*

Chapter 5
Part I: Using Prior Knowledge and Contextual Clues
Below are the sentences in which the vocabulary words appear in the text. Read the sentence. Use any clues you can find in the sentence combined with your prior knowledge, and write what you think the italicized word means in the space provided.

1. *Warily*, moving with utmost caution, Mafatu crept out of the house.

2. Warily, moving with utmost *caution*, Mafatu crept out of the house.

3. The jungle had never seemed so dark, so ominous with *peril*.

4. She was as *fleet* and gracile as the following gulls.

5. She was as fleet and *gracile* as the following gulls.

6. Their moto tabu had been *profaned* by a stranger.

7. Then the wind freshened. Just a puff, but enough. Under its *impetus* the little canoe skimmed ahead while the boy's heart gave an upward surge of thanks.

8. In that moment he was aware that the chanting of his pursuers had become fainter, steadily *diminishing*.

9. The boy quenched his thirst, ate a scrap of poi, fought against sleep as the night *waxed* and waned.

10. The boy quenched his thirst, ate a scrap of poi, fought against sleep as the night waxed and *waned*.

11. He scarcely dared now, at night, to *lash* his steering paddle and sleep.

Prereading Vocabulary Worksheets *Call It Courage*

Chapter 5, continued
Part II: Match the vocabulary words to their dictionary definitions.

_____ 1. warily   A. tie something to another object
_____ 2. caution   B. increased; enlarged
_____ 3. peril   C. forward motion; movement
_____ 4. fleet   D. gracefully slender
_____ 5. gracile   E. danger
_____ 6. profaned   F. cautiously
_____ 7. impetus   G. decreased; got smaller
_____ 8. diminishing   H. becoming smaller
_____ 9. waxed   I. showed disrespect for gods or a religion
_____ 10. waned   J. moving quickly and lightly
_____ 11. lash   K. care, close attention

ANSWER SHEET PREREADING VOCABULARY WORKSHEETS
Call It Courage

Chapter 1	Chapter 2	Chapter 3
1.	1.	1.
2.	2.	2.
3.	3.	3.
4.	4.	4.
5.	5.	5.
6.	6.	6.
7.	7.	7.
8.	8.	8.
9.	9.	9.
10.	10.	10.
11.	11.	11.
12.	12.	12.
13.		
14.		

Chapter 4	Chapter 5
1.	1.
2.	2.
3.	3.
4.	4.
5.	5.
6.	6.
7.	7.
8.	8.
9.	9.
10.	10.
	11.

ANSWER SHEET KEY PREREADING VOCABULARY WORKSHEETS
Call It Courage

Chapter 1	Chapter 2	Chapter 3
1. F	1. G	1. I
2. I	2. A	2. G
3. L	3. K	3. D
4. E	4. E	4. L
5. A	5. L	5. C
6. M	6. B	6. K
7. J	7. J	7. F
8. B	8. F	8. J
9. N	9. D	9. H
10. H	10. I	10. A
11. C	11. H	11. B
12. K	12. C	12. E
13. G		
14. D		

Chapter 4	Chapter 5
1. C	1. F
2. G	2. K
3. I	3. E
4. D	4. J
5. H	5. D
6. A	6. I
7. J	7. C
8. F	8. H
9. E	9. B
10. B	10. G
	11. A

DAILY LESSON PLANS

Daily Lesson Plans *Call It Courage*

LESSON ONE

Objectives
1. To introduce the *Call It Courage* unit
2. To distribute books, study guides and other related materials
3. To give students background information about the ancient Polynesian inhabitants of the South Seas Islands
4. To discuss the idea of "courage"
5. To discuss the characteristics of a legend

Activity #1
 Distribute books, study guides, and reading assignments. Explain in detail how students are to use these materials.

 Study Guides Students should preview the study guide questions before each reading assignment to get a feeling for what events and ideas are important in that section. After reading the section, students will (as a class or individually) answer the question to review the important events and ideas from that section of the book. Students should keep the study guides as study materials for the unit test.

 Reading/Writing Assignment Sheet You (the teachers) need to fill in the reading and writing assignment sheet to let students know when their reading has to be completed. You can either write the assignment sheet on a side blackboard or bulletin board and leave it there for students to see each day, or you can duplicate copies for each student to have. In either case, you should advise students to become very familiar with the reading and writing assignments so they know what is expected of them.

 Unit Outline You may find it helpful to distribute copies of the Unit Outline to your students so they can keep track of upcoming lessons and assignments. You may also want to post a copy of the Unit Outline on a bulletin board and cross off each lesson as you complete it.

 Extra Activities Center The Extra Activities Packet portion of this unit contains suggestions for a library of related books and articles in your classroom as well as crossword and word search puzzles. Make an extra activities center in your classroom where you will keep these materials for students to use. Bring the books and articles in from the library and keep several copies of the puzzles on hand. Explain to students that these materials are available for students to use when they finish reading assignments or other class work early.

 Books Each school has its own rules and regulations regarding student use of school books. Advise students of the procedures that are normal for your school.

Daily Lesson Plans *Call It Courage*

LESSON ONE, continued

<u>Notebook or Unit Folder</u> You may want the students to keep all of their worksheets, notes, and other papers for the unit together in a binder or notebook. During the first class meeting, tell them how you want them to arrange the folder. Make divider pages for vocabulary worksheets, prereading study guide questions, review activities, notes, and tests. You may want to give a grade for accuracy in keeping the folder.

Activity #2

Ask students to tell you what they know about the ancient Polynesians as well as the book *Call It Courage*. Do a group KWL with students. The form is included in this unit plan. Put any information the students know in the K column (What I Know.) Ask students what they want to find out and put those questions in the W column (What I Want to Find Out.) Keep the KWL sheet and refer back to it while reading. After reading the novel, complete the L column (What I Learned.)

Activity #3

Find the island of Hikueru on a map. It is part of the French Polynesian Atolls in the Pacific Ocean. Provide background about the South Seas islands, including Hikueru, Tahiti, and Bora Bora. This could be in the form of a travel video, a group search of informational web sites, or travel brochures. Invite any students who have visited the islands, or have relatives who have been there, to share their experiences. (Amazon.com carries videos about Tahiti & Samra, Bora Bora, and others in a Globe Trekker series. If you know of other sources, please submit them on our web site.)

Activity #4

Draw a concept web on the board and write the word "courage" in the center circle. Ask students to give examples that show how they think of the word courage and write them on the concept web. Ask students what they think the main character in the book might do to show his courage.

Activity #5

Read aloud the first paragraph of Chapter 1, where the author says that "the people of Hikueru sing this story in their chants and tell it over the evening fires." Explain to students that this type of story is a legend, and has certain characteristics.
- A legend is a fictional story from a particular cultural group.
- It is usually passed on from generation to generation, many times orally.
- The legend has information about the culture and its values.
- It contains a message for those who listen.

Tell students to look for the elements of a legend as they read.

KWL
Call It Courage

Directions: Before reading, think about what you already know about *Call It Courage* and/or *ancient Polynesian cultures.* Write the information in the **K** column. Think about what you would like to find out from reading the book. Write your questions in the **W** column. After you have read the book, use the **L** column to write the answers to your questions from the W column, and anything else you remember from the book.

K What I Know	W What I Want to Find Out	L What I Learned

Daily Lesson Plans *Call It Courage*

LESSON TWO

Objectives
1. To do the prereading work for Chapter 1
2. To read Chapter 1
3. To become acquainted with the Nonfiction Assignment

Activity #1

Show students how to preview the study questions and do the vocabulary work for Chapter 1. Encourage students to take notes as they read. If students own their books, encourage them to use highlighters or colored pens to mark important passages and the answers to the study guide questions.

Activity #2

Read the first two pages of Chapter 1 aloud to students to set the mood for the novel. Then have students read the remainder of the chapter orally. Either call on students or ask for volunteers, whichever works best with your class. Be sure to give students who need practice reading orally the opportunity to do so, even if it slows down the reading schedule a little. If you have not given students a grade for oral reading this quarter, during the reading of this novel would be a good time to grade them. Be sure to let them know that they will be evaluated and tell them the criteria you will use.

If students do not complete reading this assignment in class, they should finish it on their own time prior to the next class period.

Activity #3

Distribute copies of the Nonfiction Assignment Sheet and go over it in detail with the students. Explain to students that they each are to read at least one nonfiction piece at some time during the unit. Topic suggestions are included on the Extra Activities page in the Unit Resource Materials section of this manual. The nonfiction piece could be a book, a magazine article, or information from an encyclopedia or the Internet. Students will fill out a Nonfiction Assignment Sheet after completing the reading to help you (the teacher) evaluate their reading experiences and to help the students think about and evaluate their own reading. Encourage students to read about topics that are related to the theme of the novel.

NONFICTION ASSIGNMENT SHEET *Call It Courage*
(To be completed after reading the required nonfiction article.)

Name _____ Date _____ Class _____

Title of Nonfiction Read _____

Written by _____ Publication Date _____

Web Site Address (if applicable) _____

I. Factual Summary: Write a summary of the piece you read.

II. Vocabulary:
    1. Which vocabulary words were difficult?

    2. What did you do to help yourself understand the words?

III. Interpretation: What was the main point the author wanted you to get from reading his/her work?

IV. Criticism:
    1. Which points of the piece did you agree with or find easy to believe? Why?

    2. Which points of the piece did you disagree with or find difficult to believe? Why?

V. Personal Response:
    1. What did you think about this piece?

    2. How does this piece help you understand the novel *Call It Courage*?

Daily Lesson Plans *Call It Courage*

LESSON THREE

Objectives
1. To review the main ideas and events from Chapter 1
2. To do the prereading work and reading for Chapter 2
2. To give students the opportunity to practice reading orally
3. To give the teacher the opportunity to evaluate students' reading skills

Activity #1

Give students time to answer the study guide questions from Chapter 1 and then discuss the answers in detail. Write the answers on the board or overhead projector film so students can have the correct answers for study purposes.

Note: It is a good practice in public speaking and leadership skills for individual students to take charge of leading the discussion of the study questions. Perhaps a different student could go to the front of the class and lead the discussion each day that the study questions are discussed during the unit.

Activity #2

Give students about ten or fifteen minutes to complete the prereading vocabulary worksheet and preview the study guide questions for Chapter 2.

Activity #3

Tell students their oral reading ability will be evaluated. Show them copies of the Oral Reading Evaluation form and discuss it. Model correct intonation and expression by reading the first few paragraphs of Chapter 2 aloud.

Activity #4

Call on individual students to read a few paragraphs aloud. Encourage the other students to follow along in their books. If you have a student who is unwilling or unable to read aloud in front of the group, make arrangements to do his or her evaluation privately at another time. Mark the oral reading evaluation forms as the students read. If all students have read orally before the chapters have been completed, assign the remainder of the text as individual silent reading.

ORAL READING EVALUATION *Call It Courage*

Name _____ Class _____ Date _____

SKILL	EXCELLENT	GOOD	AVERAGE	FAIR	POOR
FLUENCY	5	4	3	2	1
CLARITY	5	4	3	2	1
AUDIBILITY	5	4	3	2	1
PRONUNCIATION	5	4	3	2	1
_____	5	4	3	2	1
_____	5	4	3	2	1
TOTAL GRADE	5	4	3	2	1

COMMENTS:

Daily Lesson Plans *Call It Courage*

LESSON FOUR

Objectives
1. To review the main events and ideas in Chapter 2
2. To identify the types of conflict in the novel

Activity #1
Have partners answer the study guide questions and review their prereading vocabulary worksheets. Go over the answers with the class. Then have partners write a few additional questions about the chapters. Have each pair read their questions aloud to the class and call on other students to answer.

Activity #2
Tell students that conflict is one of the most important aspects of a work of fiction. The conflict usually is an obstacle to the main character's goal. It usually brings about some type of change in the main character. The types of conflict that are evident in *Call It Courage* are character vs. nature, character vs. character, character vs. himself, and characters vs. society.

You may want to use examples from stories the students have previously read, or examples from literature for younger children to illustrate various types of conflict. Dorothy in *The Wizard of Oz* has a conflict with nature because the tornado takes her away from her home. The conflict between Cinderella and her wicked step-mother is an example of character-vs.-character conflict. In *The Little Engine That Could*, the little engine is not sure of its ability to take the train over the mountain, illustrating the character vs. himself conflict. The Greek myth of Atalanta illustrates character vs. society. Atalanta was expected to marry the man her father chose, but did not wish to do so.

Have students begin to fill out the Conflict Chart after they have read Chapters 1 and 2. Discuss their findings. Encourage them to look for more examples of conflict as they read. Tell them they will discuss conflict again as they read more of the book.

CONFLICT TRAITS CHART *Call It Courage*

Directions: Use the chart below to record examples of the different types of conflict you read about in *Call It Courage*.

CONFLICT	EXAMPLE and PAGES	CHANGE IN MAFATU
Character vs. Nature		
Character vs. Self		
Character vs. Society		
Character vs. Character		

Daily Lesson Plans *Call It Courage*

LESSON FIVE

Objectives
1. To write to express a personal opinion
2. To get the students to think about what courage and fear mean
3. To give the teacher the opportunity to evaluate students' writing

Activity #1

Write the word *opinion* on the board and ask students what it means. Invite them to give their opinions based on topics such as what should be served for lunch in the school cafeteria, if the school should have a dress code, or their favorite singer/song/group. Ask other students to agree or disagree, and state their reasons. Make the point that all people have opinions. A person expressing an opinion should be able to back it up with facts and reasons why he/she has the opinion.

Read a few letters to the editor or other nonfiction pieces that include opinions. Ask students to identify the opinions and the facts that support it.

Activity #2

Distribute Writing Assignment #1 and discuss the directions in detail. Allow students the remainder of the class period to work on this assignment. Give students an additional two or three class periods to complete the assignment if necessary.

Activity #2

Explain to students that during Lesson Seven you will be holding individual writing conferences about this writing assignment. Make sure they are familiar with the criteria on the Writing Evaluation Form.

WRITING ASSIGNMENT #1 *Call It Courage*
Writing to Express a Personal Opinion

PROMPT
You are a young person the same age as Mafatu, a member of his tribe living on the island of Hikueru. You have known Mafatu all of your life. Although you do not remember the hurricane that took his mother's life and left him afraid of the sea, you have heard the story repeatedly from others. Recently several of the other young people have shared their opinion with you that Mafatu is a coward and is bringing bad luck to the group. You see how they treat him. They ask you what you think of Mafatu. You share your opinion of him, what it means to be courageous, and also what it means to be a coward.

PREWRITING
Remember that a personal opinion piece should include your thoughts and feelings. Support these thoughts and feelings with factual evidence or examples.

First, read through the early chapters of the book to find examples of the way that Mafatu was treated. You may also want to do some additional reading on the ancient Polynesians' beliefs about courage and fear.

Make a concept web with the word *courageous* in the center. Write down any words or phrases that come to mind. Repeat the activity and make a concept web for the word *coward*. Refer to these ideas as you write.

DRAFTING
Since this assignment is meant to be spoken, your writing style can be more informal than usual. Explain your opinion in the first few sentences. Back up your opinion with personal experience or facts. Write your first draft. Check to make sure you are including your opinion. Use as many descriptive words and images as you can. You may want to use a thesaurus to help you get a variety of words and their exact meanings.

PEER CONFERENCE/REVISING
When you finish the rough draft of your personal opinion piece, ask another student to read it. After reading your rough draft, the student should tell you what he/she liked best about your work, which parts were difficult to understand, and ways in which your work could be improved. Your reader should also be able to summarize your opinion about Mafatu based on your text. Reread your text considering your critic's comments, and make the revisions you think are necessary.

PROOFREADING/EDITING
Do a final proofreading of your opinion paper, double-checking your grammar, spelling, organization, and the clarity of your ideas.

FINAL DRAFT
Follow your teacher's directions for making a final copy.

WRITING EVALUATION FORM *Call It Courage*

Name _____ Date _____ Class _____

Writing Assignment # _____

Circle One for Each Item:

Composition	Excellent	Good	Fair	Poor
Style	Excellent	Good	Fair	Poor
Grammar	Excellent	Good	Fair	Poor
Spelling	Excellent	Good	Fair	Poor
Punctuation	Excellent	Good	Fair	Poor
Legibility	Excellent	Good	Fair	Poor

Strengths:

Weaknesses:

Comments/Suggestions:

Daily Lesson Plans *Call It Courage*

LESSON SIX

Objectives
1. To do the prereading work for Chapter 3
2. To read Chapter 3
3. To complete the Study Guide questions

Activity #1
Give students about ten or fifteen minutes to complete the prereading vocabulary worksheets and to go over the study guide questions.

Activity #2
Give students the rest of the period to read the chapter and answer the study guide questions. Allow them to work individually, with a partner, or in small groups.

*Remind students to add information to their Conflict Charts as they read.

*Tell students they will have a quiz on Chapters 1, 2, and 3 in two more class periods. Encourage them to complete all prereading vocabulary and study guide pages.

Daily Lesson Plans *Call It Courage*

LESSON SEVEN

Objectives
1. To review the main ideas and events in Chapter 3
2. To participate in a writing conference with the teacher
3. To revise Writing Assignment #1 based on the teacher's suggestions
4. To prepare for a quiz on Chapters 1, 2, and 3

Activity #1
Review the study guide questions and answers for Chapter 3 with students. Then have students work with partners to write a few additional questions about the chapter. Have each pair read their questions aloud and let them call on other students to answer the questions.

Activity #2
Tell students they will have a quiz on Chapters 1, 2, and 3 during the next class period. Suggest that they go through their study guides and notes to see if they are missing any information, and to use their notes to study for the quiz.

Activity #3
Call students individually to your desk or some other private area of the classroom. Discuss their papers from Writing Assignment #1. Use the completed Writing Evaluation form as a basis for your critique.

Activity #4
Students should use their class time (when they are not in conference with you) to do any of the following: study for the quiz; work on their nonfiction reading assignment; revise Writing Assignment #1 after their conference with you; complete any reading they have not already done.

Daily Lesson Plans *Call It Courage*

LESSON EIGHT

Objectives
1. To check to see that students have done the required reading
2. To complete the prereading work for Chapter 4
3. To read Chapter 4

Activity #1
Quiz-Distribute quizzes (multiple choice study questions for Chapters 1, 2, and 3) and give students about twenty-five minutes to complete them. Correct and grade the papers as a class. You may want to have students exchange papers, or allow them to correct their own work. As an extra credit assignment, have students find the correct answers to any questions they missed, and rewrite any "false" answers to be true. Collect the quizzes for recording the grades.

Activity #2
Divide the class into small groups. Have the members of each group work together to do the prereading and vocabulary work for Chapter 4. Group members can decide how they want to approach the work. Suggest that they may want to assign a few vocabulary words to each member, and have each member teach those vocabulary words to the rest of the group. Or, they may have each member work independently, then gather as a group to go over the vocabulary words.

Activity #3
Tell students to stay in the same groups they formed to complete Activity #2. Have them sit in a small circle and take turns reading aloud quietly. As they come to the answer to one of the study guide questions, they should stop, discuss the answer, and write their response.

Daily Lesson Plans *Call It Courage*

LESSON NINE

Objectives
1. To review the main ideas and events from Chapter 4
2. To understand character traits and development by discussing Mafatu's character

Activity #1

Have students sit in small groups to discuss and answer the study questions for Chapter 4. Tell each group to choose a spokesperson. Discuss the answers to the study guide questions with the class, having each spokesperson respond for their group.

Activity #2

Explain that an author creates a character, in this case Mafatu, by giving him traits such as physical attributes, thoughts, and feelings. The author develops these traits by telling and showing what the character says, does, things, and feels. Writers usually base their characters at least in part on a real person or persons, and then elaborate. A good writer will make the characters believable for the readers.

Tell students that Armstrong Sperry grew up listening to his great-grandfather's tales about the South Sea islands and cannibals. As an adult, Sperry spent several months on the South Sea islands, including Tahiti and Bora Bora. He interacted with the native inhabitants and learned about their culture. This experience helped him develop the character of Mafatu.

Work with students to make a list of character traits on the board, such as brave, cowardly, dependable, honest, selfish, etc.

Distribute copies of the Character Traits Chart (included). Have students look back through the first four chapters and begin filling in the chart together. Tell them they should continue to be aware of Mafatu's character as they read the rest of the book, and that they will continue the discussion and complete the chart during Lesson Fifteen.

CHARACTER TRAITS CHART *Call It Courage*

CHARACTER: _____

Character Trait: _____ Events/Actions That Show the Trait:	Character Trait: _____ Events/Actions That Show the Trait:
Character Trait: _____ Events/Actions That Show the Trait:	Character Trait: _____ Events/Actions That Show the Trait:

Daily Lesson Plans *Call It Courage*

LESSON TEN

Objectives
1. To practice writing to persuade
2. To delve deeper into the character and situation of Mafatu

Activity #1
Distribute Writing Assignment #2. Discuss the directions in detail and give students ample time to complete the assignment.

Activity #2
You may want to allow students to work with partners for this assignment. If so, give them the entire class period to write.

LESSON ELEVEN

Objectives
1. To complete the prereading work for Chapter 5
2. To read Chapter 5
3. To review the main ideas and events from Chapter 5

Activity #1
Have partners preview the study questions and complete the vocabulary work for Chapter 5 together.

Activity #2
Have students work with the same partner to read Chapter 5. Tell them to take turns reading aloud. Suggest that they stop after a few pages to orally summarize what they have read, and to answer the pertinent study guide questions.

Activity #3
Review the study guide questions and answers for Chapter 5 with students. Then have students work with their partners to write a few additional questions about the chapters. Have each pair read their questions aloud and let them call on students to answer the questions.

WRITING ASSIGNMENT #2 *Call It Courage*
Writing to Persuade

PROMPT
In Chapter 1 the reader learns about the ancient Polynesians' worship of courage. The reader also learns that the main character, Mafatu, has been afraid of the sea since he was with his mother during a hurricane, and she was killed. The other members of his tribe did not like the fact that he was afraid. But instead of turning to violence toward him, they became indifferent.

Take the point of view of one person from the tribe who sees Mafatu differently. Develop a talk to persuade the others to treat Mafatu better and to find ways to help him get over his fear without driving him off the island.

PREWRITING
Make a list of reasons you think the people should treat Mafatu better. Think of statements to support each of your reasons, and list them under each reason. Then number the reasons in order from most to least important. Make a second list of suggestions for helping him overcome his fear without driving him off the island.

DRAFTING
Make an introductory statement in which you describe the problem and the supposed reasons for the way the tribe members treat Mafatu. Then briefly outline how the treatment has affected Mafatu. Next, state your request.

Then use one paragraph for each of the reasons you think the other members of his tribe should treat him better and help him get over his fear. Use the supporting statements for each reason. Make suggestions for ways they can help him. Summarize your ideas and respectfully ask for a response from a member of the community by a certain date.

PEER CONFERENCING/REVISING
When you finish the rough draft, ask another student to look at it. You may want to give the student your checklist and notes so he/she can double check for you and see that you have included all of your reasons and suggestions. After reading, the student should tell you what he/she liked best about your persuasive talk, which parts were difficult to understand or needed more information, and ways in which your work could be improved. Reread your talk considering your critic's comments and make the corrections you think are necessary.

PROOFREADING/EDITING
Do a final proofreading of your persuasive talk, double-checking your grammar, spelling, organization, and the clarity of your ideas.

FINAL DRAFT
Follow your teacher's guidelines for completing the final draft of your paper.

Daily Lesson Plans *Call It Courage*

LESSON TWELVE

Objective
To discuss *Call It Courage* at the interpretive and critical levels.

Activity #1
Choose the questions from the Extra Writing Assignments/Discussion Questions which seem most appropriate for your students. A class discussion of these questions is most effective if students have been given the opportunity to formulate answers to the questions prior to the discussion. To this end, you may either have all the students formulate answers to all the questions, divide the class into groups and assign one or more questions to each group, or you could assign one question to each student in your class. The option you choose will make a difference in the amount of class time needed for this activity.

Activity #2
After students have had ample time to answer the questions, begin your class discussion of the questions and the ideas presented by the questions. Be sure students take notes during the discussion so they have the information to study for the unit test.

EXTRA WRITING ASSIGNMENTS / DISCUSSION QUESTIONS
Call It Courage

Interpretive
1. Explain why the title of the novel is appropriate.
2. Explain why each chapter title of the novel is appropriate.
3. From what point of view is the story written? How does this affect your understanding of the story?
4. What are the main conflicts in the story? How are they resolved?
5. On the first page of the story the author says, "They worshipped courage, those early Polynesians." What does this mean?
6. What is the high point of the story? Why do you think so?
7. What is the overall mood of the book? Give examples to support your answer.
8. Discuss the imagery used in the book. How vivid is it? How effective is it?
9. What is the setting? How important is the setting to the story?
10. Is there symbolism present when the storm takes everything from Mafatu? What is it?
11. Are the characters in *Call It Courage* stereotypes? If so, explain the usefulness of employing stereotypes in *Call It Courage*. If they are not, explain how they merit individuality.
12. Describe Armstrong Sperry's writing style.

Critical
13. What is Kivi's role in the story?
14. What is Kana's role in the story?
15. What is Uri's role in the story?
16. What is an allegory, and could *Call It Courage* be considered one?
17. Why does Mafatu run away to a distant island instead of staying on Hikueru and proving to the other villagers that he was brave?
18. Mafatu befriends a bird that was a misfit. What does this tell you about his character? Why is this action symbolic in the story?
19. Discuss the theme of overcoming fear as it is presented in the novel.
20. Plot Mafatu's growth as a person throughout the novel. How did Mafatu change over the course of the story?
21. Discuss the importance of the eaters-of-men in the story.

Critical/Personal Response
22. Is the story of Mafatu's adventures believable? Explain why or why not.
23. Why do you think the author gives Mafatu a spear instead of another weapon?
24. Which event is Mafatu's greatest victory? Why?
25. Was Mafatu's journey brave or foolish? Explain your answer.
26. In Chapter 1 Mafatu thinks about going to a distant island and making his way with the people there, then returning home. How might his ideas have changed if he knew that he might land on an uninhabited island?
27. The book ends with Mafatu returning home, yet falling into his father's arms as he leaves the canoe. How effective is this ending? How else might the author have ended the story?
28. Explain why *Call It Courage* would have been popular to Sperry's audience in 1940 when it was first published.

Extra Writing Assignments/Discussion Questions, continued
Call It Courage

Personal Response

28. Did you enjoy reading *Call It Courage?* Explain why or why not.
29. Which scene or event in the story did you like the most? Why?
30. Which scene or event is the most upsetting or disturbing? Why?
31. Before you read the book, did you think it would be possible for a fifteen-year-old boy to live alone on an island? What do you think after reading *Call It Courage?*
32. Did Mafatu's experiences change the way you look at yourself? How?
33. What did you learn about the ancient Polynesian culture from reading this book?
34. Does the author's presentation of the situation make it real for you?
35. Have you read any other stories similar to *Call It Courage?* If so, tell about them.
36. Would you recommend this book to another student? Why or why not?
37. If you could change one thing about the book, what would it be?
38. What questions would you like to ask the author?
39. This book won the Newbery Award in 1942. Do you think it deserves an award? Why or why not?
40. Do you think *Call It Courage* could win the Newbery Award today? Compare and contrast *Call It Courage* to a recent Newbery winner to explain your answer.
41. Imagine that you are a young member of Mafatu's tribe, hearing this legend for the first time. What is your response to the story?

QUOTATIONS
Call It Courage

Discuss the significance of the following quotations from *Call It Courage*.

1. So the people drove him forth. Not by violence, but by indifference.

2. Mafatu's father heard the whispers, and the man grew silent and grim.

3. "Listen," they would mock. "Moana, the Sea God, thunders on the reef. He is angry with us all because Mafatu is afraid!"

4. In the air it achieved perfection, floating serenely against the sky while Mafatu followed its effortless flight with envious eyes.

5. "My father brought back word from the reef today. Already there are many bonitos out there. Tomorrow we boys will go after them. That's our job. It will be fun, eh?"

6. "Wait, Kana! I'll go! I'll try–"

7. "Ho! That is woman's work. Mafatu is afraid of the sea. *He* will never be a warrior."

8. "I have tried to be friendly with him. But he is only good for making spears. Mafatu is a coward."

9. "We're going away, Uri," he whispered fiercely. "Off to the south there are other islands."

10. *Maui é! E matai tu!"*

11. He was naked, defenseless, without food or weapon, hurled forward on the breath of the hurricane.

12. "Uri we're alive! It wasn't all a bad dream. It really happened."

13. "I will make a necklace for myself from the tusks. And when I return to Hikueru men will look at me and say: 'There goes Mafatu. He killed the wild boar single-handed!'"

14. "I must find a tree, a tamanu, for my canoe."

15. "Maui, God of the Fishermen, hear me! I shall return home one day, I swear it. My father, Tavana Nui, will be filled with pride at my homecoming. It is a vow that I take now, O Maui. I have spoken."

16. "It is you, Maui, who have helped me! My thanks, my thanks to you!"

17. "Uri, we're rich. Come–help me drag these bones home!"

Call It Courage Quotations, continued

18. "Wait, you. Wait until I have my knife. You will not be so brave then, Ma'o. You will run away when you see it flash."

19. "Today I will not go. It takes too long."

20. "A fine one you are! Where were you when I needed you? Off chasing butterflies, that's you! Was it for this I saved you from the teeth of the *ma'o*? I've a mind not to give you one mouthful of *puaa*."

21. "Taaroa, Mighty One! / My thanks to you/In this task completed. / Guide it on your back/To safe harbor. / Taaroa, *e*!"

22. Maui *é!* Do not desert me. This is the last time–lend me your help."

23. "Not yet, Moana. You haven't won. Not yet."

24. "Moana, you Sea God! You! You destroyed my mother. Always you have tried to destroy me. Fear of you has haunted my sleep. Fear of you turned my people against me. But now, now I no longer fear you, Sea!"

25. "My father, I have come home."

26. "Here is my son come home from the sea. Mafatu, Stout Heart. A brave name for a brave boy!"

Daily Lesson Plans *Call It Courage*

LESSON THIRTEEN

Objectives
1. To write to inform
2. To consider more thoroughly how Mafatu survived and what he did during his quest

Activity #1

Distribute Writing Assignment #3 and discuss the directions in detail. Allow the remaining class time for students to work on the assignment. Tell students they should finish the assignment at home and assign a date for them to turn it in.

>NOTE: This writing assignment can be done by individuals, with partners, or as a small group.

Activity #2

Decide how to present the writing assignments. You may want to set up a display area and let students read each other's guides during their free time. Or, you may want students to present their survival guides to the class. You could use some of the time allotted for Lessons 18, 19, or 20 for this work.

WRITING ASSIGNMENT 3 *Call It Courage*
Writing to Inform

PROMPT

In *Call It Courage*, you read about many things that Mafatu did to survive alone on an uninhabited island. He succeeded and returned home to Hikueru to tell the other members of his tribe about his adventures. Now you will take the persona of Mafatu and write a survivor's guide for members of his and other native Polynesian tribes.

PREWRITING

Reread the book and make a list of the things that Mafatu did to survive. Write them down in the order in which Mafatu did them. Then decide if that particular order is necessary, or if doing things in another order would work as well.

DRAFTNG

Plan the organization for your survival guide. You may want to write it according to what someone should do on Day 1, Day 2, etc., or by category, such as food, clothing, shelter. Figure out the approximate number of pages that you want for your guide. Think about the kinds of photographs and/or illustrations that you want. Give some thought to the format of the text; some of the information may be better presented in charts or as a bulleted list instead of in paragraph form.

You may want to try out a few formats before you settle on a final one. If you use a computer and word processing software, it will be easy to experiment with moving text and arranging pictures.

PEER CONFERENCING/REVISING

When you finish the rough draft, ask another student to read it. After reading the rough draft, your peer reviewer should tell you what he/she liked best about the survival guide, which parts were difficult to understand, and ways in which your work could be improved. Reread your text considering your critic's comments, and make the revisions you think are necessary.

PROOFREADING/EDITING

Do a final proofreading of your information piece, double checking your spelling, grammar, organization, and the clarity of your ideas.

FINAL DRAFT

Follow your teacher's guidelines for completing the final draft of your survival guide.

Daily Lesson Plans *Call It Courage*

LESSON FOURTEEN

<u>Objectives</u>
 To review all of the vocabulary work done in this unit

VOCABULARY REVIEW ACTIVITIES

1. Divide your class into two teams and have an old-fashioned spelling or definition bee.

2. Give individuals or groups of students a *Call It Courage* Vocabulary Word Search Puzzle with a word list. The person (group) to find all of the vocabulary words in the puzzle first wins.

3. Give students a *Call It Courage* Vocabulary Word Search Puzzle without the word list. The person or group to find the most vocabulary words in the puzzle wins.

4. Put a *Call It Courage* Vocabulary Crossword Puzzle onto a transparency on the overhead projector and do the puzzle together as a class.

5. Give students a *Call It Courage* Vocabulary Matching Worksheet to do.

6. Use words from the word jumble page and have students spell them correctly, then use them in original sentences.

7. Have students write a story in which they correctly use as many vocabulary words as possible. Have students read their compositions orally. Post the most original compositions on your bulletin board.

8. Have students work in teams and play charades with the vocabulary words.

9. Select a word of the day and encourage students to use it correctly in their writing and speaking vocabulary.

10. Have a contest to see which students can find the most vocabulary words used in other sources. You may want to have a bulletin board available so the students can write down their word, the sentence it was used in, and the source.

11. Assign a word to each student. Have them look up the origin of the word, the part of speech, definition, a synonym, and an antonym. Then have them write a sentence using the word. Have students present their information orally to the class.

Daily Lesson Plans *Call It Courage*

LESSON FIFTEEN

Objectives
1. To complete and review the Character Traits Chart
2. To complete and review the Conflict Chart
3. To review the main events and ideas of *Call It Courage*

Activity #1

Ask students to share their Character Traits Charts with the class. Encourage students to add information from other students to their charts. If students have different ideas about Mafatu's character traits, allow time for them to discuss their ideas. Tell students to keep their charts and use them while studying for the Unit Test.

Activity #2

Review the Conflict Charts with the class. Make sure students understand the different types of conflicts and have selected the appropriate examples of each from the text. Tell students to keep their charts and use them while studying for the Unit Test.

Activity #3

Choose one of the review games/activities included in this packet and spend your class time as outlined there.

Activity #4

Remind students of the date of the unit test. Stress the review of the study guides and their class notes as a last minute, brush-up review.

REVIEW GAMES/ACTIVITIES *Call It Courage*

1. Ask the class to make up a unit test for *Call It Courage* (including a separate answer key). The test should have 4 sections: multiple choice, true/false, short answer, and essay. Students may use 1/2 period to make the test with a separate answer key and then swap papers and use the other 1/2 class period to take a test a classmate has devised (open book). You may want to use the unit test included in this packet or take questions from the students' unit tests to formulate your own test.

2. Take 1/2 period for students to make up true and false questions (including the answers). Collect the papers, and divide the class into two teams. Draw a big tic-tac-toe board on the chalkboard. Make one team X and one team O. Ask questions to each side, giving each student one turn. If the question is answered correctly, that students' team's letter (X or O) is placed in the box. If the answer is incorrect, no mark is placed in the box. The object is to get three marks in a row like tic-tac-toe. You may want to keep track of the number of games won for each team.

3. Take 1/2 period for students to make up questions (true/false and short answer). Collect the questions. Divide the class into two teams. You'll alternate asking questions to individual members of teams A & B (like in a spelling bee). The question keeps going from A to B until it is correctly answered, then a new question is asked. A correct answer does not allow the team to get another question. Correct answers are +2 points; incorrect answers are -1 point.

4. Allow students time to quiz each other (in pairs or small groups) from their study guides and class notes.

5. Give students a *Call It Courage* crossword puzzle to complete.

6. Divide your class into two teams. Use the *Call It Courage* crossword words with their letters jumbled as a word list. Student 1 from Team A faces off against Student 1 from Team B. You write the first jumbled word on the board. The first student (1A or 1B) to unscramble the word wins the chance for his/her team to score points. If 1A wins the jumble, go to student 2A and give him/her a clue. He/she must give you the correct word which matches that clue. If he/she does, Team A scores a point, and you give student 3A a clue for which you expect another correct response. Continue giving Team A clues until some team member makes an incorrect response. An incorrect response sends the game back to the jumbled-word face off, this time with students 2A and 2B.

7. Take on the persona of "The Answer Person." Allow students to ask any question about the book. Answer the questions, or tell students where to look in the book to find the answer.

Review Activities *Call It Courage*, continued

8. Students may enjoy playing charades with events from the story. Select a student to start. Give him/her a card with a scene or event from the story. Allow the players to use their books to find the scene being described. The first person to guess each charade performs the next one.

9. Play a categories-type quiz game. (A master is included in this manual). Make an overhead transparency of the categories form. Divide the class into teams of three or four players each. Have each team Choose a recorder and a banker. Choose a team to go first. That team will choose a category and point amount. Ask the question to the entire class. (Use the Study Guide Quiz and Vocabulary questions.) Give the teams one minute to discuss the answer and write it down. Walk around the room and check the answers. Each team that answers correctly receives the points. (Incorrect answers are not penalized; they just don't receive any points). Cross out that square on the playing board. Play continues until all squares have been used. The winning team is the one with the most points. You can assign bonus points to any square or squares you choose.

10. Have individual students draw scenes from the book. Display the scenes and have the rest of the class look in their books to find the chapter or section that is being depicted. The first student to find the correct scene then displays his or her picture. When the game is over, collect the pictures and put them in a binder for students to look at during their free time.

11. Have students create a survival kit, either with real materials or pictures. Include an explanation of why each item is necessary. Display the survival kit in the classroom.

NOTE: If students do not need the extra review, omit this lesson and go on to the test.

QUIZ GAME *Call It Courage*

Chapter 1	Chapter 2	Chapter 3	Chapter 4	Chapter 5
100	100	100	100	100
200	200	200	200	200
300	300	300	300	300
400	400	400	400	400
500	500	500	500	500

Daily Lesson Plans *Call It Courage*

LESSON SIXTEEN

Objective
To test the students understanding of the main ideas, themes, and events in *Call It Courage*

Activity #1
Distribute *Call It Courage* tests. Discuss the directions in detail and allow students the entire class period to complete the test. If they finish this segment early, they may continue to work on their "take home" essays (Writing Assignment #3) until the end of the period.

Activity #2
Collect all test papers and assigned books prior to the end of the period.

NOTES ABOUT THE UNIT TESTS IN THIS UNIT:

There are 5 different unit tests which follow.

There are two short answer tests which are based primarily on facts from the novel. The answer key for short answer unit test 1 follows the student test. The answer key for short answer test 2 follows the student short answer unit test 2.

There is one advanced short answer unit test. It is based on the extra discussion questions. Use the matching key for short answer unit test 2 to check the matching section of the advanced short answer unit test. There is no key for the short answer questions. The answers will be based on the discussions you have had during class.

There are two multiple choice unit tests. Following the two unit tests, you will find an answer sheet on which students should mark their answers. The same answer sheet should be used for both tests; however, students' answers will be different for each test. Following the students' answer sheet for the multiple choice tests you will find your two keys: one for multiple-choice test 1 and one for multiple choice test 2.

The short answer tests have a vocabulary section. You should choose 10 of the vocabulary words from this unit, read them orally and have the students write them down. Then, either have students write a definition or use the words in sentences. The second part of the vocabulary test is matching.

Daily Lesson Plans *Call It Courage*

LESSON SEVENTEEN

Objectives
1. To widen the breadth of students' knowledge about the topics discussed or touched upon in *Call It Courage*
2. To present the nonfiction assignments

Activity #1
Ask each student to give a brief oral report about the nonfiction work he/she read for the nonfiction assignment. Your criteria for evaluating this report will vary depending on the level of your students. You may wish for students to give the complete report without using notes of any kind. Or you may want students to read directly from a written report. You may want to do something between these two options. Make students aware of your criteria in ample time for them to prepare their reports.

Start with one student's report. After that, ask if anyone else in the class has read on a topic related to the first student's report. If no one has, choose another student at random. After each report, be sure to ask if anyone has a report related to the one just completed. That will help keep continuity during the discussion of the reports.

Activity #2
Collect the students' written reports. Put them in a binder and have the binder available for all students to read.

Activity #3
If the class or school has a Web site, post the nonfiction reports there.

Daily Lesson Plans *Call It Courage*

LESSON EIGHTEEN

Objective
> To complete a project associated with *Call It Courage* to further explore the book from a different perspective

Activity #1
> Assign one of the projects below, or allow students to choose one. Give students class time to work on the project.

Project 1
> Think about something which has recently happened to you where you had to show courage. Imitate Armstrong Sperry's style, and write about your experience as a legend that might be told around the campfire or around the school in years to come. After writing your story, practice reciting it. Then give an oral presentation of your story.

Project 2
> Choose one scene from *Call It Courage* and rewrite it as a play. Perform the play for the class. Then, explain the difficulties, if any, you encountered in doing so.

Project #3
> Rewrite one scene or chapter of *Call It Courage* as a graphic novel. Publish your version on poster board and show it to the class.

Project #4
> Design your own project. Explain why you want to do your project and how it is relevant to the themes in *Call It Courage*.

LESSON NINETEEN

Objective
> To complete a project associated with *Call It Courage*

Activity #1
> Continue working on the projects for the entire class period. This may take more than one class period.

LESSON TWENTY

Objective
> To present a project associated with *Call It Courage*

Activity #1
> Present the completed projects to the class. Invite students to share constructive comments about each other's work. This may take more than one class period.

UNIT TESTS

SHORT ANSWER UNIT TEST 1 *Call It Courage*

I. Matching/Identification

____ 1. KANA   A. Paths of the sea; ocean currents used by Polynesians: ____ *Moana*

____ 2. KIVI   B. This at the base of the tree trunk helped Mafatu fell the tree for his canoe.

____ 3. WHALE   C. This skeleton was used for making tools.

____ 4. SHARK   D. Mafatu killed it by slitting its belly open with his knife.

____ 5. EATERS   E. ____-of-men chased Mafatu.

____ 6. TAHITI   F. Grandfather who told about the Smoking Islands

____ 7. COCONUT G. Island where Mafatu thought he would arrive

____ 8. FIRE   H. Deformed albatross & Mafatu's companion

____ 9. ARA   I. Youth who was friendly to Mafatu

____ 10. RUAU   J. Mafatu used its leaves to build a lean-to and drank its juice.

____ 11. RAFT   K. Mafatu built one so he could set fish traps.

____ 12. MOANA   L. The Sea God

II. Short Answer
Directions: Answer each question.

1. What is the setting of the story? Include the time, the place, and the name of the group of people.

2. What does Mafatu fear and why?

Short Answer Unit Test 1, *Call It Courage*

3. What happens to Mafatu and his canoe during the storm in his journey away from Hikueru?

4. What does Mafatu do when he reaches land?

5. What vow does Mafatu make, and to whom does he make it?

6. What does Mafatu discover at the end of the trail on the island? What does he do when he arrives at the end of the trail?

Short Answer Unit Test 1, *Call It Courage*

7. Describe how and why Mafatu kills the hammerhead shark. Include how Mafatu feels.

8. Describe what happens to Mafatu's knife while he is out fishing. Include what he does about the knife.

9. What does Mafatu do when the eaters-of-men go after him?

10. Describe Mafatu's homecoming.

Short Answer Unit Test 1, *Call It Courage*

III. Quotations
Directions: Identify the speaker or situation and discuss the significance of each quotation.

1. So the people drove him forth. Not by violence, but by indifference.

2. "My father brought back word from the reef today. Already there are many bonitos out there. Tomorrow we boys will go after them. That's our job. It will be fun, eh?"

3. "Maui, God of the Fishermen, hear me! I shall return home one day, I swear it. My father, Tavana Nui, will be filled with pride at my homecoming. It is a vow that I take now, O Maui. I have spoken."

4. "Today I will not go. It takes too long."

5. "My father, I have come home."

Short Answer Unit Test 1, *Call It Courage*

IV: Essay

Discuss the theme of overcoming fear as it is presented in the novel.

Short Answer Unit Test 1, *Call It Courage*

V. Vocabulary Part 1
   Listen to the vocabulary word and spell it. After you have spelled all the words, go back and write down the definitions.

WORD	DEFINITION
1. _____	_____
2. _____	_____
3. _____	_____
4. _____	_____
5. _____	_____
6. _____	_____
7. _____	_____
8. _____	_____
9. _____	_____
10. _____	_____

Vocabulary Part 2: Place the letter of the matching definition on the blank line.

_____ 1. apprehension   A. showed disrespect for gods or a religion
_____ 2. caution   B. lack of interest or concern
_____ 3. dismal   C. noisy uproar
_____ 4. fierce   D. mocked by shouting or laughing
_____ 5. indifference   E. depressing
_____ 6. jeered   F. contempt; disrespect
_____ 7. profaned   G. worry; nervousness
_____ 8. scorn   H. formed; created
_____ 9. tumult   I. ferocious; violent
_____ 10. wrought   J. care, close attention

ANSWER KEY: SHORT ANSWER UNIT TEST I *Call It Courage*

I -	1. KANA	A. Paths of the sea; ocean currents used by Polynesians: ___ *Moana*
H -	2. KIVI	B. This at the base of the tree trunk helped Mafatu fell the tree for his canoe.
C -	3. WHALE	C. This skeleton was used for making tools.
D -	4. SHARK	D. Mafatu killed it by slitting its belly open with his knife.
E -	5. EATERS	E. ___-of-men chased Mafatu.
G -	6. TAHITI	F. Grandfather who told about the Smoking Islands
J -	7. COCONUT	G. Island where Mafatu thought he would arrive
B -	8. FIRE	H. Deformed albatross & Mafatu's companion
A -	9. ARA	I. Youth who was friendly to Mafatu
F -	10. RUAU	J. Mafatu used its leaves to build a lean-to and drank its juice.
K -	11. RAFT	K. Mafatu built one so he could set fish traps.
L -	12. MOANA	L. The Sea God

II. Short Answer
Directions: Answer each question.

1. What is the setting of the story? Include the time, the place, and the name of the group of people.
   The story is set many years ago in the South Sea Islands. The people are Polynesians who live on the island/atoll of Hikueru.

2. What does Mafatu fear and why?
   Mafatu is afraid of the sea. When he was three, there was a great hurricane. Mafatu was out in a reef pool in a canoe with his mother. The canoe was carried out to sea. The canoe capsized and the two were carried to a small island. The mother saved the boy but she died.

3. What happens to Mafatu and his canoe during the storm in his journey away from Hikueru?
   A huge wave lifts the canoe and washes away all of Mafatu's possessions, including his clothing or *pareu*. The wave also destroys the canoe's sail and mast.

4. What does Mafatu do when he reaches land?
   He drags himself to the edge of the jungle collapses on the bank of the stream.

Answer Key Short Answer Unit Test 1, *Call It Courage*

5. What vow does Mafatu make, and to whom does he make it?
    Mafatu vows to Maui, the God of the Fishermen, that he will return to his father, Tavana Nui.

6. What does Mafatu discover at the end of the trail on the island? What does he do when he arrives at the end of the trail?
    He discovers a sacred place that belongs to the eaters-of-men. He also sees a spearhead, and, in spite of his fear, he takes the spearhead from the sacred platform.

7. Describe how and why Mafatu kills the hammerhead shark. Include how Mafatu feels.
    Mafatu and Uri go out in the raft to set the fishing traps. Uri falls off the raft when a wave goes across the reef. The shark goes after Uri and Mafatu dives into the water. He is already angry at the shark for destroying the fish trap. Now is he in a rage because the shark is attacking his dog. Mafatu swims under the shark and stabs it in the belly. He kills the shark and Uri is unharmed. When he gets back to shore, Mafatu feels humble with gratitude. He realizes that he was able to kill the shark because of his feelings for the dog.

8. Describe what happens to Mafatu's knife while he is out fishing. Include what he does about the knife.
    Mafatu is fishing in his new canoe when the knife falls overboard. He wants to get the knife, but it is deep down on the bottom of the sea and he has never dived that far. Also, he would have to dive past holes where the giant octopus might live. Mafatu decides to dive and gets his knife. On his swim back to the surface an octopus attacks him. He uses his knife to stab the octopus in both eyes, killing it. He keeps the body and plans to show the tentacles to the people at home.

9. What does Mafatu do when the eaters-of-men go after him?
    He runs to his canoe, gets in, and takes off.

10. Describe Mafatu's homecoming.
    The people gather on the shore as the canoe comes in. No one recognizes Mafatu when he gets out and walks onto the beach. Then he greets his father. When his father realizes that this stranger is his son, he tells the people the boy's name is Stout Heart.

III. Quotations
Directions: Identify the speaker or situation and discuss the significance of each quotation.

1. So the people drove him forth. Not by violence, but by indifference.
    This line from the story describes how the other islanders treated Mafatu after it became clear that he was afraid of the sea.

Answer Key Short Answer Unit Test 1, *Call It Courage*

2. "My father brought back word from the reef today. Already there are many bonitos out there. Tomorrow we boys will go after them. That's our job. It will be fun, eh?"
    Kana said this to Mafatu. He was trying to see if Mafatu would have the courage to go out with the other boys to fish.

3. "Maui, God of the Fishermen, hear me! I shall return home one day, I swear it. My father, Tavana Nui, will be filled with pride at my homecoming. It is a vow that I take now, O Maui. I have spoken."
    Mafatu made this promise soon after he arrived on the island.

4. "Today I will not go. It takes too long."
    Every day Mafatu climbed the plateau to look out to sea and search for the canoes of the eaters-of-men. He knew he had to be ready to leave before they came. On this day, he was tired from working on his canoe and thought he would not make the climb. In the end, however, he did climb the plateau. This is when he killed the wild boar.

5. "My father, I have come home."
    Mafatu says this when he walks onto the shore of Hikueru. None of the villagers, including his father, have recognized him.

IV: Essay

Discuss the theme of overcoming fear as it is presented in the novel.

(For Teacher Notes)

Answer Key Short Answer Unit Test 1, *Call It Courage*

V. Vocabulary Part 1
Listen to the vocabulary word and spell it. After you have spelled all the words, go back and write down the definitions.

	WORD	DEFINITION
1.	_____	_____
2.	_____	_____
3.	_____	_____
4.	_____	_____
5.	_____	_____
6.	_____	_____
7.	_____	_____
8.	_____	_____
9.	_____	_____
10.	_____	_____

Vocabulary Part 2: Place the letter of the matching definition on the blank line.

G   1. apprehension   A. showed disrespect for gods or a religion
J   2. caution   B. lack of interest or concern
E   3. dismal   C. noisy uproar
I   4. fierce   D. mocked by shouting or laughing
B   5. indifference   E. depressing
D   6. jeered   F. contempt; disrespect
A   7. profaned   G. worry; nervousness
F   8. scorn   H. formed; created
C   9. tumult   I. ferocious; violent
H   10. wrought   J. care, close attention

SHORT ANSWER UNIT TEST 2 *Call It Courage*

I. Matching/Identification
Directions: Place the letter of the matching definition on the blank line.

____ 1. KANA	A. ____-of-men chased Mafatu.

____ 2. CANOE	B. Color of Mafatu's dog

____ 3. BANANA	C. Mafatu built one for his trip home.

____ 4. EATERS	D. Youth who was friendly to Mafatu

____ 5. YELLOW	E. Chief; Mafatu's father: ____ Nui

____ 6. HURRICANE	F. Killed Mafatu's mother

____ 7. FIFTEEN	G. Island where Mafatu thought he would arrive

____ 8. BOAR	H. Mafatu's age when he went off by himself

____ 9. TAHITI	I. Mafatu made a necklace with ____'s teeth.

____10. FIRE	J. This at the base of the tree trunk helped Mafatu fell the tree for his canoe.

____11. MULBERRY	K. This tree's bark lining was used to make clothing.

____12. TAVANA	L. This tree's fruit had been cut off recently.

II. Short Answer
Directions: Answer each question.

1. How do the older people treat Mafatu? What do they believe was at fault for his problem?

2. One night the main character overhears Kana, one of the other boys, make a comment. What is the comment, how does the main character feel about it, and what does the main character do in response?

Short Answer Unit Test 2, *Call It Courage*

3. Describe the land that Mafatu sees in the distance when he is in his canoe.

4. Which god does Mafatu think has carried him safely across the water?

5. What survival-related actions does Mafatu take during his early days on the island?

6. While he is on the island, what does Mafatu discover about the tasks he did in Hikueru?

Short Answer Unit Test 2, *Call It Courage*

7. What does Mafatu use to make a new *pareu* to wear? Why is it important for him to have this article of clothing?

8. Describe how Mafatu kills the wild boar. Include how he feels about this accomplishment and what he does afterwards.

9. Describe Mafatu's journey home, starting with him seeing the eaters-of-men on the island.

10. Describe Mafatu's homecoming.

Short Answer Unit Test 2, *Call It Courage*

III. Quotations
Directions: Identify the speaker and discuss the significance of each quotation.

1. "Taaroa, Mighty One!/ My thanks to you/In this task completed./ Guide it on your back/To safe harbor./ Taaroa, *e*!"

2. He was naked, defenseless, without food or weapon, hurled forward on the breath of the hurricane.

3. "Listen," they would mock. "Moana, the Sea God, thunders on the reef. He is angry with us all because Mafatu is afraid!"

4. "A fine one you are! Where were you when I needed you? Off chasing butterflies, that's you! Was it for this I saved you from the teeth of the *ma'o*? I've a mind not to give you one mouthful of *puaa*."

5. "Uri, we're rich. Come–help me drag these bones home!"

Short Answer Unit Test 2, *Call It Courage*

IV: Essay

Discuss Mafatu's growth as a person throughout the novel.

Short Answer Unit Test 2, *Call It Courage*

V. Vocabulary Part 1
   Listen to the vocabulary word and spell it. After you have spelled all the words, go back and write down the definitions.

   WORD   DEFINITION

1. _____   _____

2. _____   _____

3. _____   _____

4. _____   _____

5. _____   _____

6. _____   _____

7. _____   _____

8. _____   _____

9. _____   _____

10. _____   _____

Vocabulary Part 2: Place the letter of the matching definition on the blank line.

_____ 1. convulsively   A. a feeling of extraordinary happiness
_____ 2. cauterize   B. walls of a fort
_____ 3. elation   C. tie something to another object
_____ 4. fleet   D. noisy uproar
_____ 5. grotesque   E. lack of interest or concern
_____ 6. indifference   F. bizarre; gross
_____ 7. lash   G. seal a wound with something that burns
_____ 8. pinnacle   H. top; highest point
_____ 9. ramparts   I. moving quickly and lightly
_____ 10. tumult   J. in a violently jerking or shaking manner

ANSWER KEY: SHORT ANSWER UNIT TEST 2 *Call It Courage*

I. Matching/Identification
Directions: Place the letter of the matching definition on the blank line.

D -	1. KANA	A.	___-of-men chased Mafatu.
C -	2. CANOE	B.	Color of Mafatu's dog
L -	3. BANANA	C.	Mafatu built one for his trip home.
A -	4. EATERS	D.	Youth who was friendly to Mafatu
B -	5. YELLOW	E.	Chief; Mafatu's father: ___ Nui
F -	6. HURRICANE	F.	Killed Mafatu's mother
H -	7. FIFTEEN	G.	Island where Mafatu thought he would arrive
I -	8. BOAR	H.	Mafatu's age when he went off by himself
G -	9. TAHITI	I.	Mafatu made a necklace with ___'s teeth.
J -	10. FIRE	J.	This at the base of the tree trunk helped Mafatu fell the tree for his canoe.
K -	11. MULBERRY	K.	This tree's bark lining was used to make clothing.
E -	12. TAVANA	L.	This tree's fruit had been cut off recently.

II. Short Answer
Directions: Answer each question.

1. How do the older people treat Mafatu? What do they believe was at fault for his problem?
   The older people treat Mafatu well. They think the *tupapau*, or ghost-spirit that is in every child at birth is at fault for his fear.

2. One night the main character overhears Kana, one of the other boys, make a comment. What is the comment, how does the main character feel about it, and what does the main character do in response?
   Kana is talking with the other boys. He says that they will all go out the next day to look for food—all except Mafatu, who is a coward. Mafatu feels resentment and decides he must prove his courage to himself and the group. He must go out and face Moana, the Sea God.

Answer Key Short Answer Unit Test 2, *Call It Courage*

3. Describe the land that Mafatu sees in the distance when he is in his canoe.
    The land has a high mountain with trees growing from the shoreline.

4. Which god does Mafatu think has carried him safely across the water?
    He thinks it was Maui, the God of the Fishermen.

5. What survival-related actions does Mafatu take during his early days on the island?
    He squeezes lime juice into the cut on his leg and wraps a bandage of *purau* leaves on it. He discovers a sacred place that belongs to the eaters-of-men. He also sees a spearhead, and, in spite of his fear, he takes the spearhead from the sacred platform. He makes a fire, cooks breadfruit and bananas for his and Uri's dinner, plaits some coconut fronds into screens, and chooses a tree to use for a canoe.

6. While he is on the island, what does Mafatu discover about the tasks he did in Hikueru?
    He finds out that the tasks, such as making nets and knives and fishhooks, are all things he needs to know now in order to survive. He is glad he has the skills to make the things he needs.

7. What does Mafatu use to make a new *pareu* to wear? Why is it important for him to have this article of clothing?
    He uses the fibers of a mulberry tree to make the *pareu*. It is important for him to be well clothed when he returns home. He wants the others to realize that he has conquered the sea and land.

8. Describe how Mafatu kills the wild boar. Include how he feels about this accomplishment and what he does afterwards.
    Mafatu is climbing the trail to the top of the mountain when he hears noise in the underbrush. As the wild boar charges, Mafatu aims his spear. He kills the boar and makes a sled of bamboo to drag the dead animal down to his camp. There, he roasts the meat and makes a necklace of the tusks. When he puts on the necklace, he feels the magic of the boar making him strong.

9. Describe Mafatu's journey home, starting with him seeing the eaters-of-men on the island.
    The sound of drums wakes him. He realizes the drums belong to the eaters-of-men who are returning to the island. When he climbs to his lookout, he sees that the eaters-of-men are on the island and they are dancing at their sacred place. Then he sees four of the men running towards him. He runs to his canoe, gets in, and takes off. The eaters-of-men have six canoes that go after Mafatu. The wind is in his favor and he stays ahead. They chase him all day and into the night. Then the warriors begin falling behind. By dawn the next morning he does not hear or see them. The winds hold for several days, then die down. Mafatu paddles on, and begins to see sharks. In frustration he shouts at Moana, the Sea God. Suddenly he sees a lagoon fire and realizes that Hikueru is just ahead of him. Kivi is in the air above him.

Answer Key Short Answer Unit Test 2, *Call It Courage*

10. Describe Mafatu's homecoming.
    The people gather on the shore as the canoe comes in. No one recognizes Mafatu when he gets out and walks onto the beach. Then he greets his father. When his father realizes that this stranger is his son, he tells the people the boy's name is Stout Heart.

III. Quotations

Directions: Identify the speaker and discuss the significance of each quotation.

1. "Taaroa, Mighty One!/ My thanks to you/In this task completed./ Guide it on your back/To safe harbor./ Taaroa, *e*!"
    Mafatu is on the island when he says this. He has finished making his canoe and says the prayer that all of the fishermen on Hikueru say when they launch their ships.

2. He was naked, defenseless, without food or weapon, hurled forward on the breath of the hurricane.
    This is the way the author describes Mafatu during the storm that occurs during his voyage to the island. A huge wave destroyed the mast and sail of the canoe and swept away all of his clothes and provisions.

3. "Listen," they would mock. "Moana, the Sea God, thunders on the reef. He is angry with us all because Mafatu is afraid!"
    Mafatu's stepbrothers and stepmother would mockingly say this about him.

4. "A fine one you are! Where were you when I needed you? Off chasing butterflies, that's you! Was it for this I saved you from the teeth of the *ma'o*? I've a mind not to give you one mouthful of *puaa*."
    Mafatu says this to Uri. Mafatu has just killed the wild boar while Uri was nowhere in sight to help. Now Uri comes out of the jungle and sees Mafatu with the dead boar.

5. "Uri, we're rich. Come–help me drag these bones home!"
    Mafatu says this to Uri when he finds the whale skeleton on the beach. He realizes that now he has the supplies he needs to make tools, including a knife.

IV: Essay

Discuss Mafatu's growth as a person throughout the novel.

(For Teacher Notes)

Answer Key Short Answer Unit Test 2, *Call It Courage*

V. Vocabulary Part 1

Listen to the vocabulary word and spell it. After you have spelled all the words, go back and write down the definitions.

	WORD	DEFINITION
1.		
2.		
3.		
4.		
5.		
6.		
7.		
8.		
9.		
10.		

Vocabulary Part 2: Place the letter of the matching definition on the blank line.

J	1. convulsively	A. a feeling of extraordinary happiness
G	2. cauterize	B. walls of a fort
A	3. elation	C. tie something to another object
I	4. fleet	D. noisy uproar
F	5. grotesque	E. lack of interest or concern
E	6. indifference	F. bizarre; gross
C	7. lash	G. seal a wound with something that burns
H	8. pinnacle	H. top; highest point
B	9. ramparts	I. moving quickly and lightly
D	10. tumult	J. in a violently jerking or shaking manner

Advanced Short Answer Unit Test, *Call It Courage*

I. Matching/Identification
Directions: Place the letter of the matching definition on the blank line.

____ 1. KANA   A. ___-of-men chased Mafatu.

____ 2. CANOE   B. Color of Mafatu's dog

____ 3. BANANA   C. Mafatu built one for his trip home.

____ 4. EATERS   D. Youth who was friendly to Mafatu

____ 5. YELLOW   E. Chief; Mafatu's father: ___ Nui

____ 6. HURRICANE   F. Killed Mafatu's mother

____ 7. FIFTEEN   G. Island where Mafatu thought he would arrive

____ 8. BOAR   H. Mafatu's age when he went off by himself

____ 9. TAHITI   I. Mafatu made a necklace with ____'s teeth.

____ 10. FIRE   J. This at the base of the tree trunk helped Mafatu fell the tree for his canoe.

____ 11. MULBERRY   K. This tree's bark lining was used to make clothing.

____ 12. TAVANA   L. This tree's fruit had been cut off recently.

II. Short Answer
Directions: Answer each question.

1. Explain the significance of each chapter title of the novel.

2. Which event is Mafatu's greatest victory? Use examples from the book to support your answer.

Advanced Short Answer Unit Test, *Call It Courage*

3 What are the main conflicts in the story? How are they resolved?

4. Discuss the theme of overcoming fear as it is presented in the novel.

5. What survival-related actions does Mafatu take during his days on the island? Explain these in detail. Start with his arrival on the island and include his actions up to his departure. Explain how each action helps Mafatu grow in courage and self-sufficiency.

Advanced Short Answer Unit Test, *Call It Courage*

III. Quotations
Directions: Identify the speaker and discuss the significance of each quotation.

1. So the people drove him forth. Not by violence, but by indifference.

2. "My father brought back word from the reef today. Already there are many bonitos out there. Tomorrow we boys will go after them. That's our job. It will be fun, eh?"

3. "Maui, God of the Fishermen, hear me! I shall return home one day, I swear it. My father, Tavana Nui, will be filled with pride at my homecoming. It is a vow that I take now, O Maui. I have spoken."

4. "Today I will not go. It takes too long."

5. "My father, I have come home."

Advanced Short Answer Unit Test, *Call It Courage*

III. Quotations, continued

6. "Taaroa, Mighty One! / My thanks to you/In this task completed. / Guide it on your back/To safe harbor. / Taaroa, *e*!"

7. He was naked, defenseless, without food or weapon, hurled forward on the breath of the hurricane.

8. "Listen," they would mock. "Moana, the Sea God, thunders on the reef. He is angry with us all because Mafatu is afraid!"

9. "A fine one you are! Where were you when I needed you? Off chasing butterflies, that's you! Was it for this I saved you from the teeth of the *ma'o*? I've a mind not to give you one mouthful of *puaa*."

10. "Uri, we're rich. Come–help me drag these bones home!"

Advanced Short Answer Unit Test, *Call It Courage*

<u>IV. Vocabulary</u>
Directions: Listen to the words and write them down. After you have written down all of the words, write a paragraph in which you use all of the words. The paragraph must in some way relate to the book *Call It Courage*.

MULTIPLE CHOICE UNIT TEST 1 *Call It Courage*

I. Matching/Identification: Directions: Match the term and its meaning.

____ 1. FOUR   A. Occupation of the villagers

____ 2. MULBERRY   B. Island of Mafatu's home

____ 3. FISHING   C. The Boy Who Was Afraid

____ 4. CANOE   D. Mafatu made this from whale bone

____ 5. KNIFE   E. Mafatu feared this.

____ 6. SPEARHEAD   F. Mafatu made new clothing to show he had conquered the ___.

____ 7. SEA   G. Mafatu built one for his trip home.

____ 8. LAND   H. Number of eaters-of-men who chased Mafatu on the island

____ 9. MAFATU   I. This tree's bark lining was used to make clothing.

____10. URI   J. Mafatu stole it from the statue.

____11. MAUI   K. Canine companion to Mafatu

____12. HIKUERU   L. God of the Fishermen

II. Multiple Choice

1. What is the setting of the story?
    A. The story is set in 1865 in Gettysburg, Pennsylvania.
    B. The story is set in modern-day Hawaii.
    C. The story is set on the island of Sicily in the 1500s.
    D. The story is set many years ago in the South Sea Islands.

2. What does Mafatu fear and why?
    A. Mafatu is afraid of the dark because he has poor eyesight.
    B. Mafatu is afraid of boats because he cannot swim.
    C. Mafatu is afraid of the sea because his mother died in a hurricane.
    D. Mafatu is afraid of the other children because he is the smallest one.

3. What happens to Mafatu's canoe during the storm?
    A. The wave destroys the canoe's sail and mast.
    B. A wave breaks the canoe into pieces.
    C. A wave spins the canoe in circles.
    D. Nothing; the canoe is safe during the storm.

Multiple Choice Unit Test 1 *Call It Courage*

4. What does Mafatu hear when he reaches the sand?
    A. He hears children playing games on the beach.
    B. He hears his dog barking.
    C. He hears the wind blowing through the trees.
    D. He hears the sound of fresh, running water.

5. Mafatu makes a vow to _____.
    A. live alone on the island for five years
    B. offer sacrifices to the gods every day
    C. never feel afraid again
    D. return to his father

6. What does Mafatu do at the sacred platform?
    A. He takes the spearhead from the sacred platform.
    B. He gets down on his knees and prays to the statue he sees.
    C. He buries all of the bones he finds lying around.
    D. He destroys the statue in anger.

7. Mafatu kills the _____ when it goes after Uri.
    A. wild boar
    B. giant rattlesnake
    C. hammerhead shark
    D. pack of vultures

8. Mafatu kills the _____ when he dives into the water to search for his knife.
    A. manta ray
    B. octopus
    C. electric eel
    D. hammerhead shark

9. When Mafatu climbs to the top of the plateau, he sees _____ running towards him.
    A. five large, pale-skinned sailors
    B. a pack of wild dogs
    C. four eaters-of-men
    D. his dog, Uri

10. True or False: No one recognizes Mafatu when he reaches the shore.
    A. True
    B. False

Multiple Choice Unit Test 1 *Call It Courage*

III. Quotations
Directions: Match the two parts of each quotation.

1. So the people drove him forth.

2. "Listen," they would mock. "Moana, the Sea God, thunders on the reef.

3. "My father brought back word from the reef. Already there are many bonitos out there.

4. "I shall return home one day, I swear it. My father, Tavana Nui, will be filled with pride at my homecoming.

5. "Today I will not go.

6. Wait, you. Wait until I have my knife. You will not be so brave then, Ma'o.

7. "Where were you when I needed you? Off chasing butterflies, that's you!

8. "Here is my son come home from the sea. Mafatu, Stout Heart.

9. Maui *é!* Do not desert me.

10. "I will make a necklace for myself from the tusks.

A. You will run away when you see it flash."

B. He is angry with us all because Mafatu is afraid!"

C. This is the last time–lend me your help."

D. Tomorrow we boys will go after them. That's our job. It will be fun, eh?"

E. Was it for this I saved you from the teeth of the *ma'o*? I've a mind not to give you one mouthful of *puaa.*"

F. And when I return to Hikueru men will look at me and say: 'There goes Mafatu. He killed the wild boar single-handed!'"

G. It is a vow that I take now, O Maui. I have spoken."

H. A brave name for a brave boy!"

I. Not by violence, but by indifference.

J. It takes too long."

Multiple Choice Unit Test 1 *Call It Courage*

IV. Vocabulary Part 1 Directions: Match the word and its meaning.
1. apprehension   A. showed disrespect for gods or a religion
2. caution   B. lack of interest or concern
3. dismal   C. noisy uproar
4. fierce   D. mocked by shouting or laughing
5. indifference   E. depressing
6. jeered   F. contempt; disrespect
7. profaned   G. worry; nervousness
8. scorn   H. formed; created
9. tumult   I. ferocious; violent
10. wrought   J. care, close attention

Vocabulary Part 2 Directions: Mark the letter next to the word that matches the definition.

11. increased; enlarged
    A. waxed
    B. waned
    C. capsized
    D. congealed

12. bizarre; gross
    A. taut
    B. pinnacle
    C. grotesque
    D. indifference

13. rough; incomplete
    A. irresolute
    B. rude
    C. taut
    D. lash

14. trembling or shrinking back with fear
    A. tantalizing
    B. quailing
    C. wrought
    D. luminous

15. brave, sturdy
    A. gracile
    B. inevitable
    C. livid
    D. stout

16. very angry
    A. luminous
    B. oppressive
    C. livid
    D. scorn

17. danger
    A. peril
    B. fierce
    C. dismal
    D. fleet

18. impossible to prevent from happening
    A. grotesque
    B. irresolute
    C. pinnacle
    D. inevitable

19. someone responsible for a misdeed
    A. missionaries
    B. culprit
    C. mutter
    D. profaned

20. strengthen by encouraging
    A. bolster
    B. cauterize
    C. adze
    D. siphoned

MULTIPLE CHOICE UNIT TEST 2 *Call It Courage*

I. Matching/Identification: Directions: Match the term and its meaning.

____ 1. TAHITI   A. Island where Mafatu thought he would arrive

____ 2. GHOST   B. Uninhabited islet where Mafatu and his mother landed

____ 3. MULBERRY   C. Mafatu built one so he could set fish traps.

____ 4. CORAL   D. Mafatu feared this.

____ 5. FIFTEEN   E. Mafatu's age when he went off by himself

____ 6. SEA   F. This tree's bark lining was used to make clothing.

____ 7. TEKOTO   G. Killed Mafatu's mother

____ 8. SPEARHEAD   H. Tupapau or ___ spirit

____ 9. RAFT   I. It forms the reefs.

____ 10. THREE   J. Mafatu's age when his mother died

____ 11. FORBIDDEN   K. Mafatu stole it from the statue.

____ 12. HURRICANE   L. Where Mafatu landed & eaters-of-men made sacrifices: ___ Island

II. Multiple Choice

1. What do the older people believe was at fault for Mafatu's problem?
    A. They think the *tupapau,* or ghost-spirit that is in every child at birth is at fault.
    B. They think his father was mean to him and is at fault for the problem.
    C. They think he brought the problem on himself.
    D. They think his mother did not teach him correctly when he was younger.

2. One night Kana says that Mafatu is a coward. What does Mafatu realize he must do?
    A. He must challenge Kana to a fight to the death.
    B. He must move to the other side of the island and live alone.
    C. He must ignore the comment for the good of the group.
    D. He must go out and face Moana, the Sea God.

3. Describe the land that Mafatu sees in the distance when he is in his canoe.
    A. The land is flat, just like Hikueru.
    B. The land is covered with short bushes and flowers.
    C. The land has a high mountain with trees growing from the shoreline.
    D. The land is a dry, sandy desert with no plants.

Multiple Choice Unit Test 2 *Call It Courage*

4. Which god does Mafatu think has carried him safely across the water?
    A. He thinks it was Neptune, the Sea God.
    B. He thinks it was Maui, the God of the Fishermen.
    C. He thinks it was Poseidon, the Water God.
    D. He thinks it was Tuamotu, the God of Sailors.

5. Mafatu took several survival-related actions. Which of the following is **not** one of them?
    A. cooks breadfruit and bananas
    B. plaits coconut fronds into screens
    C. makes a signal fire at the top of the mountain
    D. chooses a tree to use for a canoe

6. True or False: Mafatu now realizes that the tasks he did on Hikueru, such as making nets and fishhooks, were worthless and don't help him at all now.
    A. True
    B. False

7. Mafatu wants to be well _____ when he returns home. He wants the others to realize that he has conquered the sea and land.
    A. fed
    B. rested
    C. clothed
    D. educated

8. Mafatu feels magic when he puts on his new necklace made of _____.
    A. wild boar tusks
    B. abalone shells
    C. prayer beads that he made himself
    D. plaited coconut fiber and juju vines

9. The winds hold for _____ of Mafatu's journey home.
    A. two hours
    B. the entire length
    C. several days
    D. one day

10. His father tells the people that Mafatu's name is _____.
    A. Recovers from Cowardice
    B. Killer of All Enemies
    C. He Who Wears the Boar Tusk Necklace
    D. Stout Heart

Multiple Choice Unit Test 2 *Call It Courage*

III. Quotations
Directions: Match the two parts of each quotation.

1. "Ho! That is woman's work.

2. He was naked, defenseless, without food or weapon,

3. "Maui, God of the Fishermen, hear me!

4. "Moana, the Sea God, thunders on the reef.

5. "Uri, we're rich.

6. "Taaroa, Mighty One! My thanks to you in this task completed.

7. Men will look at me and say: "There goes Mafatu.

8. Wait until I have my knife.

9. So the people drove him forth.

10. "I must find a tree,

A. He is angry with us all because Mafatu is afraid!"

B. hurled forward on the breath of the hurricane.

C. Guide it on your back to safe harbor.

D. You will run away when you see it flash. You will not be so brave then, Ma'o."

E. Mafatu is afraid of the sea. *He* will never be a warrior."

F. Not by violence, but by indifference.

G. I shall return home one day, I swear it.

H. Come–help me drag these bones home!"

I. a tamanu, for my canoe."

J. He killed the wild boar single-handed!"

Multiple Choice Unit Test 2 *Call It Courage*

IV. Vocabulary Part 1 Directions: Match the word and its meaning.

1. convulsively
2. cauterize
3. elation
4. fleet
5. grotesque
6. indifference
7. lash
8. pinnacle
9. ramparts
10. tumult

A. a feeling of extraordinary happiness
B. walls of a fort
C. tie something to another object
D. noisy uproar
E. lack of interest or concern
F. bizarre; gross
G. seal a wound with something that burns
H. top; highest point
I. moving quickly and lightly
J. in a violently jerking or shaking manner

Vocabulary Part 2 Directions: Mark the letter next to the word that matches the definition.

11. stiff; stretched tight
    A. livid
    B. oppressive
    C. taut
    D. luminous

12. decreased; got smaller
    A. waned
    B. waxed
    C. profaned
    D. siphoned

13. formed; created
    A. seized
    B. wrought
    C. lured
    D. jeered

14. a tool for cutting heavy pieces of wood
    A. scorn
    B. rampart
    C. lagoon
    D. adze

15. balanced; suspended
    A. tantalized
    B. poised
    C. cast
    D. gleamed

16. a feeling of hopelessness
    A. elation
    B. inevitable
    C. dismay
    D. exertion

17. distances between things
    A. intervals
    B. apprehension
    C. extremity
    D. impetus

18. gracefully slender
    A. tantalizing
    B. apprehension
    C. veritable
    D. gracile

19. complain indistinctly
    A. quailing
    B. rending
    C. mutter
    D. relish

20. contempt; disrespect
    A. vantage
    B. culprit
    C. bolster
    D. scorn

ANSWER SHEET MULTIPLE CHOICE UNIT TESTS *Call It Courage*

I. Matching	III. Quotations	IV. Vocabulary
1.	1.	1.
2.	2.	2.
3.	3.	3.
4.	4.	4.
5.	5.	5.
6.	6.	6.
7.	7.	7.
8.	8.	8.
9.	9.	9.
10.	10.	10.
11.		11.
12.		12.

II. Multiple Choice

1. (A) (B) (C) (D)   13.

2. (A) (B) (C) (D)   14.

3. (A) (B) (C) (D)   15.

4. (A) (B) (C) (D)   16.

5. (A) (B) (C) (D)   17.

6. (A) (B) (C) (D)   18.

7. (A) (B) (C) (D)   19.

8. (A) (B) (C) (D)   20.

9. (A) (B) (C) (D)

10. (A) (B) (C) (D)

ANSWER SHEET KEY MULTIPLE CHOICE UNIT TEST 1 *Call It Courage*

I. Matching	III. Quotations	IV. Vocabulary
1. H	1. I	1. G
2. I	2. B	2. J
3. A	3. D	3. E
4. G	4. G	4. I
5. D	5. J	5. B
6. J	6. A	6. D
7. E	7. E	7. A
8. F	8. H	8. F
9. C	9. C	9. C
10. K	10. F	10. H
11. L		11. A
12. B		12. C

II. Multiple Choice

1. (A) (B) (C) ( )
2. (A) (B) ( ) (D)
3. ( ) (B) (C) (D)
4. (A) (B) (C) ( )
5. (A) (B) (C) ( )
6. ( ) (B) (C) (D)
7. (A) (B) ( ) (D)
8. (A) ( ) (C) (D)
9. (A) (B) ( ) (D)
10. ( ) (B) (C) (D)

13. B
14. B
15. D
16. C
17. A
18. D
19. B
20. A

ANSWER SHEET KEY MULTIPLE CHOICE UNIT TEST 2 *Call It Courage*

I. Matching	III. Quotations	IV. Vocabulary
1. A	1. E	1. J
2. H	2. B	2. G
3. F	3. G	3. A
4. I	4. A	4. I
5. E	5. H	5. F
6. D	6. C	6. E
7. B	7. J	7. C
8. K	8. D	8. H
9. C	9. F	9. B
10. J	10. I	10. D
11. L		11. C
12. G		12. A

II. Multiple Choice
1. ( ) (B) (C) (D)
2. (A) (B) (C) ( )
3. (A) (B) ( ) (D)
4. (A) ( ) (C) (D)
5. (A) (B) ( ) (D)
6. (A) ( ) (C) (D)
7. (A) (B) ( ) (D)
8. ( ) (B) (C) (D)
9. (A) (B) ( ) (D)
10. (A) (B) (C) ( )

13. B
14. D
15. B
16. C
17. A
18. D
19. C
20. D

UNIT RESOURCE MATERIALS

BULLETIN BOARD IDEAS *Call It Courage*

1. Save one corner of the board for the best of students' *Call It Courage* writing assignments. You may want to use background maps to represent the setting of the novel.

2. Take one of the word search puzzles from the extra activities packet and with a marker copy it over in a large size on the bulletin board. Write the clue words to find to one side. Invite students prior to and after class to find the words and circle them on the bulletin board.

3. Have students find or draw pictures that they think resemble the people and scenery in the book.

4. Invite students to help make an interactive bulletin board quiz. Give each student a half-sheet of paper (about 4"x5") folded in half so that it can open. On the outside flap, have each student write a description of one of the characters in the text. On the inside, they will write the name of the character. You can staple or tack these papers to the bulletin board so that the students can read the descriptions and lift the flaps to find the answers.

5. Collect and display pictures of Polynesian islands and native inhabitants.

6. Display articles about the native inhabitants of the Polynesian Islands, tales of survival on deserted islands, or other tales of courage.

7. Display articles about the author, Armstrong Sperry.

8. Have students design postcards depicting the settings of the book.

EXTRA ACTIVITIES *Call It Courage*

One of the difficulties in teaching a novel is that all students don't read at the same speed. One student who likes to read may take the book home and finish it in a day or two. Sometimes a few students finish the in-class assignments early. The problem, then, is finding suitable extra activities for students.

One thing that helps is to keep a little library in the classroom. For this unit on *Call It Courage* you might check out from the school or public library other books about survival, courageous acts, hunting, diving, the Polynesian islands, sharks, tides and currents, oceanography, trapping lobsters, making canoes, types of canoes, canoeing, nutrition of fruits and fish or pork, butchering and roasting a pig, making survival tools, fishing nets and other equipment, fishing techniques, and other books set in that time frame.

Your students who have reading difficulties, or speak English as a second language may benefit from listening to all or part of the book on audiotape. *Call It Courage* is available commercially, or you may want to have an adult or a student who reads well tape record the book for you.

A Spanish language translation of the book *Call It Courage,* titled *Esto Es Coraje* is also available. Students who read Spanish fluently may enjoy reading the Spanish version as well as the English.

Other things you may keep on hand are word search puzzles. Several puzzles relating directly to *Call It Courage* are included in the unit. Feel free to duplicate them.

Some students may like to draw. You might devise a contest or allow some extra-credit grade for students who draw characters or scenes from *Call It Courage.* Note, too, that if the students do not want to keep their drawings you may pick up some extra bulletin board materials this way. If you have a contest and you supply the prize. You could, possibly, make the drawing itself a nonrefundable entry fee.

Have maps, a globe, and travel brochures on hand for easy reference. Travel agencies and automobile clubs are good sources for these materials.

The pages which follow contain games, puzzles, and worksheets. The keys, when appropriate, immediately follow the puzzle or worksheet. There are two main groups of activities: one group for the unit; that is, generally relating to the *Call It Courage* text, and another group of activities related strictly to the *Call It Courage* vocabulary.

Directions for the games, puzzles, and worksheets are self-explanatory. The object here is to provide you with extra materials you may use in any way you choose.

MORE ACTIVITIES *Call It Courage*

1. Pick one of the incidents for students to dramatize. Encourage students to write dialog for the characters. Since most of the book focuses on the one character, students could provide dialogue for the other characters who are mentioned briefly. For example, they could write about what Mafatu's father and the other villagers said and did when they discovered that he was missing. Or, they could write a dialogue among the eaters-of-men when they find that someone has trespassed on their sacred site. (Perhaps you could assign various stories to different groups of students so more than one story could be acted and more students could participate.)

2. Have students design a bulletin board (ready to be put up; not just sketched) for *Call It Courage*.

3. Invite someone to talk to the class about the concept of courage and bravery in tribal groups.

4. Have someone from a travel agency give a presentation about the Polynesian islands and its native inhabitants, including past and present history.

5. Ask someone from a scout troop or outdoors club to talk to the class about survival in the wilderness.

6. Help students design and produce a talk show. Choose one of the story incidents as the topic. The host will interview the various characters. (Students should make up the questions they want the host to ask the characters.)

7. Have students work in pairs to create an interview with one of the characters. One student should be the interviewer and the other should be the interviewee. Students can work together to compose questions for the interviewer to ask. Each pair of students could present their interview to the class. Students could include interviews with Uri the dog and Kivi the albatross, imagining what they might say if they could talk.

8. Invite students who have read other books by Armstrong Sperry to present booktalks to the class.

9. Invite students who have read other books on a similar topic as *Call It Courage* to present booktalks to the class.

10. Use some of the related topics (noted earlier for an in-class library) as topics for research, reports, or written papers, or as topics for guest speakers.

11. Invite someone who has knowledge of early Polynesian cultures to talk to the class.

MORE ACTIVITIES *Call It Courage*

12. Have students hold small group discussions related to topics in the book. Assign a recorder and a speaker for each group. Have the speaker from each group make a report to the class.

13. Use the Internet to take a virtual field trip to the site of *Call It Courage*.

14. Research the life of Armstrong Sperry.

15. Research the early Polynesian tribes, including how they made weapons and tools.

16. If possible, invite someone who has visited the Polynesian islands to talk to the class and show their pictures.

17. Bring in music from the Polynesian islands and play it for the class.

18. Write additional chapters for the book, telling what happened to Mafatu after he returned from his journey.

19. Find out how native inhabitants live in the Polynesian islands today.

20. Find out more about the history of the Newbery Medal. Find out which other authors won the medal. Get a list of the criteria used for awarding the medal. With a small group, discuss whether or not you think *Call It Courage* deserved the medal and if you think it would win today.

21. Research other books that were nominated for the Newbery Medal at the same time as *Call It Courage*. Read a few of the books and compare and contrast them with *Call It Courage*.

CALL IT COURAGE WORD SEARCH

```
L P A R E U T A V A N A I W M T G H F M
I J M F T D S T S W G V X R U A X P I X
M R Q V S M P P Z P I T J V L M C S S W
E C N Q R E B P K X Z D J B A J J H T
Y L F E S Z A G O K N I F E E N J G I J
V W F F A Q R W L L Z M D N R U Y Q N M
K M N B H T H Q Y P W R C M R F K R G T
Q S A W S R E Q N H U U H X Y Z X S T K
B C W R T M A R E M M R X I M H R E L M
A N A N A B D Z S T E I K T K L K A N A
C C P E L M S M I S G R K H A U N T T J
G J R N E M O X A O A C M R K D E L F V
R T U F R K A B N H R O O T W K M R O K
S T A H I T I U S G U C A N O E O W U X
T X U N F F T F I S O O G T L E A H R W
B P G Q K A T S G X C N O X L R N A Q R
Y O S J F R H E A R T U H R E H A L V F
Z Z A A G H X Q E C W T M F Y T F E H S
F H M R V J H N N N H U R R I C A N E R
T K N N F Q X P M F O R B I D D E N S P
```

ARA	FIFTEEN	KANA	PAREU	TAHITI
BANANA	FIRE	KIVI	POLYNESIANS	TAMANU
BOAR	FISHING	KNIFE	RAFT	TAVANA
CANOE	FORBIDDEN	LAND	RUAU	TEKOTO
COCONUT	FOUR	LIME	SEA	THREE
CORAL	GHOST	MAFATU	SHARK	URI
COURAGE	HEART	MAUI	SMOKING	WHALE
DRUMS	HIKUERU	MOANA	SPEARHEAD	YELLOW
EATERS	HURRICANE	MULBERRY	STREAM	

CALL IT COURAGE WORD SEARCH ANSWER KEY

```
L P A R E U T A V A N A I   M T       F
I                       V   U A       I
M         S             I   L M       S
E         P       P     K N I F E R   H
          E       O       D   R U     I
          A       L       R   R       N
      A   R       Y       U   Y   S   G
      R   M A R E M       I       E
  A N A N A B D   S T E   K L K A N A
      E       M I S G     R   A   T
      R   E   O A S O   K R D     E   F
  T U F R K   A N H R   C R W K M R   O
S T A H I T I U S G U C A N O E O W   U
    U N F F T I   O O N O T L E A H   R
  B G   A     E   C N U   L R N A
  O     F R H E A R T     E H A L
      A         E N H U R R I C A N E
      M R       F O R B I D D E N
```

ARA	FIFTEEN	KANA	PAREU	TAHITI
BANANA	FIRE	KIVI	POLYNESIANS	TAMANU
BOAR	FISHING	KNIFE	RAFT	TAVANA
CANOE	FORBIDDEN	LAND	RUAU	TEKOTO
COCONUT	FOUR	LIME	SEA	THREE
CORAL	GHOST	MAFATU	SHARK	URI
COURAGE	HEART	MAUI	SMOKING	WHALE
DRUMS	HIKUERU	MOANA	SPEARHEAD	YELLOW
EATERS	HURRICANE	MULBERRY	STREAM	

CALL IT COURAGE CROSSWORD

Across
2. Mafatu's age when his mother died
6. Mafatu treats his wound with ___ juice.
8. Mafatu killed it by slitting its belly open with his knife.
9. Mafatu feared this.
10. Uninhabited islet where Mafatu and his mother landed
13. Mafatu made a necklace with ____'s teeth.
14. Mafatu built one so he could set fish traps.
17. Where Mafatu landed & eaters-of-men made sacrifices: ___ Island
18. Grandfather who told about the Smoking Islands
21. Color of Mafatu's dog
23. Youth who was friendly to Mafatu
24. Mafatu's christened name: Stout ___
25. Clothing
26. This tree's fruit had been cut off recently.
27. The Sea God

Down
1. Occupation of the villagers
3. ___-of-men chased Mafatu.
4. Tupapau or ___ spirit
5. The sound of these wakes Mafatu.
6. Mafatu made new clothing to show he had conquered the ___.
7. This tree's bark lining was used to make clothing.
11. Mafatu made this from whale bone
12. God of the Fishermen
15. This at the base of the tree trunk helped Mafatu fell the tree for his canoe.
16. The Boy Who Was Afraid
17. Mafatu's age when he went off by himself
19. Mafatu collapses near one when he arrives at the island.
20. Tree used to make the canoe
22. This skeleton was used for making tools.

CALL IT COURAGE CROSSWORD ANSWER KEY

¹F				²T	H	³R	E	E	⁴G		⁵D	
I		⁶L	⁷I	M	E			A		⁸S	H	A	R	K
⁹S	E	A	U		¹⁰T	E	¹¹K	O	T	O		O		U
H		N	L		¹²M		N		E			S		M
I		D	¹³B	O	A	R		I		¹⁴R	¹⁵A	F	T	S
N			E		U			F		S		I		¹⁶M
G	¹⁷F	O	R	B	I	D	D	E	N		¹⁸R	U	A	U
	I		R					¹⁹S		E		F		²⁰T
	²¹F	Y	E	L	L	O	²²W		T		²³K	A	N	A
	T						H		R			T		M
	²⁴H	E	A	R	T		²⁵P	A	R	E	U		U		A
	E						L		A					N
²⁶B	A	N	A	N	A		²⁷E		M	O	A	N	A	U

Across
2. Mafatu's age when his mother died
6. Mafatu treats his wound with ___ juice.
8. Mafatu killed it by slitting its belly open with his knife.
9. Mafatu feared this.
10. Uninhabited islet where Mafatu and his mother landed
13. Mafatu made a necklace with ____'s teeth.
14. Mafatu built one so he could set fish traps.
17. Where Mafatu landed & eaters-of-men made sacrifices: ___ Island
18. Grandfather who told about the Smoking Islands
21. Color of Mafatu's dog
23. Youth who was friendly to Mafatu
24. Mafatu's christened name: Stout ___
25. Clothing
26. This tree's fruit had been cut off recently.
27. The Sea God

Down
1. Occupation of the villagers
3. ___-of-men chased Mafatu.
4. Tupapau or ___ spirit
5. The sound of these wakes Mafatu.
6. Mafatu made new clothing to show he had conquered the ___.
7. This tree's bark lining was used to make clothing.
11. Mafatu made this from whale bone
12. God of the Fishermen
15. This at the base of the tree trunk helped Mafatu fell the tree for his canoe.
16. The Boy Who Was Afraid
17. Mafatu's age when he went off by himself
19. Mafatu collapses near one when he arrives at the island.
20. Tree used to make the canoe
22. This skeleton was used for making tools.

CALL IT COURAGE MATCHING 1

___ 1. WHALE   A. Tupapau or ___ spirit
___ 2. RUAU   B. Home of the eaters-of-men: ___ Island
___ 3. CANOE   C. Paths of the sea; ocean currents used by Polynesians: ___ Moana
___ 4. GHOST   D. Mafatu treats his wound with ___ juice.
___ 5. ARA   E. Grandfather who told about the Smoking Islands
___ 6. TAVANA   F. God of the Fishermen
___ 7. DRUMS   G. Mafatu built one so he could set fish traps.
___ 8. KANA   H. The Boy Who Was Afraid
___ 9. PAREU   I. It forms the reefs.
___ 10. SMOKING   J. Canine companion to Mafatu
___ 11. MAUI   K. Mafatu stole it from the statue.
___ 12. KNIFE   L. Youth who was friendly to Mafatu
___ 13. HEART   M. Uninhabited islet where Mafatu and his mother landed
___ 14. MAFATU   N. Tree used to make the canoe
___ 15. MOANA   O. This tree's bark lining was used to make clothing.
___ 16. TEKOTO   P. Mafatu built one for his trip home.
___ 17. THREE   Q. Mafatu's christened name: Stout ___
___ 18. SPEARHEAD   R. Chief; Mafatu's father: ___ Nui
___ 19. MULBERRY   S. Mafatu's age when his mother died
___ 20. TAMANU   T. This skeleton was used for making tools.
___ 21. RAFT   U. Mafatu made new clothing to show he had conquered the ___.
___ 22. LIME   V. Clothing
___ 23. LAND   W. The sound of these wakes Mafatu.
___ 24. CORAL   X. Mafatu made this from whale bone
___ 25. URI   Y. The Sea God

CALL IT COURAGE MATCHING 1 ANSWER KEY

T - 1. WHALE   A. Tupapau or ___ spirit

E - 2. RUAU   B. Home of the eaters-of-men: ___ Island

P - 3. CANOE   C. Paths of the sea; ocean currents used by Polynesians: ___ Moana

A - 4. GHOST   D. Mafatu treats his wound with ___ juice.

C - 5. ARA   E. Grandfather who told about the Smoking Islands

R - 6. TAVANA   F. God of the Fishermen

W - 7. DRUMS   G. Mafatu built one so he could set fish traps.

L - 8. KANA   H. The Boy Who Was Afraid

V - 9. PAREU   I. It forms the reefs.

B -10. SMOKING   J. Canine companion to Mafatu

F -11. MAUI   K. Mafatu stole it from the statue.

X -12. KNIFE   L. Youth who was friendly to Mafatu

Q -13. HEART   M. Uninhabited islet where Mafatu and his mother landed

H -14. MAFATU   N. Tree used to make the canoe

Y -15. MOANA   O. This tree's bark lining was used to make clothing.

M -16. TEKOTO   P. Mafatu built one for his trip home.

S -17. THREE   Q. Mafatu's christened name: Stout ___

K -18. SPEARHEAD   R. Chief; Mafatu's father: ___ Nui

O -19. MULBERRY   S. Mafatu's age when his mother died

N -20. TAMANU   T. This skeleton was used for making tools.

G -21. RAFT   U. Mafatu made new clothing to show he had conquered the ___.

D -22. LIME   V. Clothing

U -23. LAND   W. The sound of these wakes Mafatu.

I -24. CORAL   X. Mafatu made this from whale bone

J -25. URI   Y. The Sea God

CALL IT COURAGE MATCHING 2

___ 1. SPEARHEAD   A. Mafatu made new clothing to show he had conquered the ___.

___ 2. KANA   B. Mafatu used its leaves to build a lean-to and drank its juice.

___ 3. COCONUT   C. Occupation of the villagers

___ 4. POLYNESIANS   D. Mafatu built one for his trip home.

___ 5. PAREU   E. Mafatu made this from whale bone

___ 6. URI   F. Color of Mafatu's dog

___ 7. HIKUERU   G. Mafatu stole it from the statue.

___ 8. EATERS   H. Mafatu's christened name: Stout ___

___ 9. RAFT   I. Chief; Mafatu's father: ___ Nui

___ 10. HEART   J. Island of Mafatu's home

___ 11. TAHITI   K. ___-of-men chased Mafatu.

___ 12. FORBIDDEN   L. This at the base of the tree trunk helped Mafatu fell the tree for his canoe.

___ 13. LAND   M. Deformed albatross & Mafatu's companion

___ 14. FISHING   N. Where Mafatu landed & eaters-of-men made sacrifices: ___ Island

___ 15. KIVI   O. Mafatu built one so he could set fish traps.

___ 16. TAMANU   P. Number of eaters-of-men who chased Mafatu on the island

___ 17. TAVANA   Q. Canine companion to Mafatu

___ 18. STREAM   R. Tree used to make the canoe

___ 19. CANOE   S. Clothing

___ 20. MULBERRY   T. Youth who was friendly to Mafatu

___ 21. FOUR   U. Mafatu collapses near one when he arrives at the island.

___ 22. YELLOW   V. This tree's bark lining was used to make clothing.

___ 23. FIRE   W. Native people who lived on the islands

___ 24. RUAU   X. Island where Mafatu thought he would arrive

___ 25. KNIFE   Y. Grandfather who told about the Smoking Islands

CALL IT COURAGE MATCHING 2 ANSWER KEY

G - 1. SPEARHEAD   A. Mafatu made new clothing to show he had conquered the ___.
T - 2. KANA   B. Mafatu used its leaves to build a lean-to and drank its juice.
B - 3. COCONUT   C. Occupation of the villagers
W - 4. POLYNESIANS D. Mafatu built one for his trip home.
S - 5. PAREU   E. Mafatu made this from whale bone
Q - 6. URI   F. Color of Mafatu's dog
J - 7. HIKUERU   G. Mafatu stole it from the statue.
K - 8. EATERS   H. Mafatu's christened name: Stout ___
O - 9. RAFT   I. Chief; Mafatu's father: ___ Nui
H - 10. HEART   J. Island of Mafatu's home
X - 11. TAHITI   K. ___-of-men chased Mafatu.
N - 12. FORBIDDEN L. This at the base of the tree trunk helped Mafatu fell the tree for his canoe.
A - 13. LAND   M. Deformed albatross & Mafatu's companion
C - 14. FISHING   N. Where Mafatu landed & eaters-of-men made sacrifices: ___ Island
M - 15. KIVI   O. Mafatu built one so he could set fish traps.
R - 16. TAMANU   P. Number of eaters-of-men who chased Mafatu on the island
I - 17. TAVANA   Q. Canine companion to Mafatu
U - 18. STREAM   R. Tree used to make the canoe
D - 19. CANOE   S. Clothing
V - 20. MULBERRY   T. Youth who was friendly to Mafatu
P - 21. FOUR   U. Mafatu collapses near one when he arrives at the island.
F - 22. YELLOW   V. This tree's bark lining was used to make clothing.
L - 23. FIRE   W. Native people who lived on the islands
Y - 24. RUAU   X. Island where Mafatu thought he would arrive
E - 25. KNIFE   Y. Grandfather who told about the Smoking Islands

CALL IT COURAGE JUGGLE LETTER REVIEW

1. OGACRUE = 1. _____
   Polynesians worshipped it.

2. AONAM = 2. _____
   The Sea God

3. AEPRU = 3. _____
   Clothing

4. ERFI = 4. _____
   This at the base of the tree trunk helped Mafatu fell the tree for his canoe.

5. EARTH = 5. _____
   Mafatu's christened name: Stout ___

6. NTUOCCO = 6. _____
   Mafatu used its leaves to build a lean-to and drank its juice.

7. ASE = 7. _____
   Mafatu feared this.

8. IREUUKH = 8. _____
   Island of Mafatu's home

9. SUDMR = 9. _____
   The sound of these wakes Mafatu.

10. VKII =10. _____
    Deformed albatross & Mafatu's companion

11. NLDA =11. _____
    Mafatu made new clothing to show he had conquered the ___.

12. TENIEFF =12. _____
    Mafatu's age when he went off by himself

13. OEKTOT =13. _____
    Uninhabited islet where Mafatu and his mother landed

14. AOENC =14. _____
    Mafatu built one for his trip home.

15. ORALC =15. _____
    It forms the reefs.

16. KSRHA =16. _____
Mafatu killed it by slitting its belly open with his knife.

17. FENIK =17. _____
Mafatu made this from whale bone

18. RULRMEBY =18. _____
This tree's bark lining was used to make clothing.

19. RSEAHDPEA =19. _____
Mafatu stole it from the statue.

20. IAUM =20. _____
God of the Fishermen

21. RIEOBDFND =21. _____
Where Mafatu landed & eaters-of-men made sacrifices: ___ Island

22. VATANA =22. _____
Chief; Mafatu's father: ___ Nui

23. UURA =23. _____
Grandfather who told about the Smoking Islands

24. UFRO =24. _____
Number of eaters-of-men who chased Mafatu on the island

25. FTAR =25. _____
Mafatu built one so he could set fish traps.

26. NANAAB =26. _____
This tree's fruit had been cut off recently.

27. INGHSFI =27. _____
Occupation of the villagers

28. RETMSA =28. _____
Mafatu collapses near one when he arrives at the island.

29. IRANERUHC =29. _____
Killed Mafatu's mother

30. TEEASR =30. _____
___-of-men chased Mafatu.

31. LEWOYL =31. _____
Color of Mafatu's dog

32. LWEAH =32. _____
This skeleton was used for making tools.

33. THREE =33. _____
Mafatu's age when his mother died

34. SGTHO =34. _____
Tupapau or ___ spirit

35. IRU =35. _____
Canine companion to Mafatu

36. ROBA =36. _____
Mafatu made a necklace with ____'s teeth.

37. ATMUAN =37. _____
Tree used to make the canoe

38. UTFMAA =38. _____
The Boy Who Was Afraid

39. ITTAHI =39. _____
Island where Mafatu thought he would arrive

40. NKAA =40. _____
Youth who was friendly to Mafatu

41. RAA =41. _____
Paths of the sea; ocean currents used by Polynesians: ___ Moana

42. NEAOSYLPISN =42. _____
Native people who lived on the islands

CALL IT COURAGE JUGGLE LETTER REVIEW ANSWER KEY

1. OGACRUE = 1. COURAGE
   Polynesians worshipped it.

2. AONAM = 2. MOANA
   The Sea God

3. AEPRU = 3. PAREU
   Clothing

4. ERFI = 4. FIRE
   This at the base of the tree trunk helped Mafatu fell the tree for his canoe.

5. EARTH = 5. HEART
   Mafatu's christened name: Stout ___

6. NTUOCCO = 6. COCONUT
   Mafatu used its leaves to build a lean-to and drank its juice.

7. ASE = 7. SEA
   Mafatu feared this.

8. IREUUKH = 8. HIKUERU
   Island of Mafatu's home

9. SUDMR = 9. DRUMS
   The sound of these wakes Mafatu.

10. VKII = 10. KIVI
    Deformed albatross & Mafatu's companion

11. NLDA = 11. LAND
    Mafatu made new clothing to show he had conquered the ___.

12. TENIEFF = 12. FIFTEEN
    Mafatu's age when he went off by himself

13. OEKTOT = 13. TEKOTO
    Uninhabited islet where Mafatu and his mother landed

14. AOENC = 14. CANOE
    Mafatu built one for his trip home.

15. ORALC = 15. CORAL
    It forms the reefs.

16. KSRHA =16. SHARK
Mafatu killed it by slitting its belly open with his knife.

17. FENIK =17. KNIFE
Mafatu made this from whale bone

18. RULRMEBY =18. MULBERRY
This tree's bark lining was used to make clothing.

19. RSEAHDPEA =19. SPEARHEAD
Mafatu stole it from the statue.

20. IAUM =20. MAUI
God of the Fishermen

21. RIEOBDFND =21. FORBIDDEN
Where Mafatu landed & eaters-of-men made sacrifices: ___ Island

22. VATANA =22. TAVANA
Chief; Mafatu's father: ___ Nui

23. UURA =23. RUAU
Grandfather who told about the Smoking Islands

24. UFRO =24. FOUR
Number of eaters-of-men who chased Mafatu on the island

25. FTAR =25. RAFT
Mafatu built one so he could set fish traps.

26. NANAAB =26. BANANA
This tree's fruit had been cut off recently.

27. INGHSFI =27. FISHING
Occupation of the villagers

28. RETMSA =28. STREAM
Mafatu collapses near one when he arrives at the island.

29. IRANERUHC =29. HURRICANE
Killed Mafatu's mother

30. TEEASR =30. EATERS
___-of-men chased Mafatu.

31. LEWOYL =31. YELLOW
Color of Mafatu's dog

32. LWEAH =32. WHALE
This skeleton was used for making tools.

33. THREE =33. THREE
Mafatu's age when his mother died

34. SGTHO =34. GHOST
Tupapau or ___ spirit

35. IRU =35. URI
Canine companion to Mafatu

36. ROBA =36. BOAR
Mafatu made a necklace with ____'s teeth.

37. ATMUAN =37. TAMANU
Tree used to make the canoe

38. UTFMAA =38. MAFATU
The Boy Who Was Afraid

39. ITTAHI =39. TAHITI
Island where Mafatu thought he would arrive

40. NKAA =40. KANA
Youth who was friendly to Mafatu

41. RAA =41. ARA
Paths of the sea; ocean currents used by Polynesians: ___ Moana

42. NEAOSYLPISN =42. POLYNESIANS
Native people who lived on the islands

Call It Courage Word List

No.	Word	Clue/Definition
1.	ARA	Paths of the sea; ocean currents used by Polynesians: ___ Moana
2.	BANANA	This tree's fruit had been cut off recently.
3.	BOAR	Mafatu made a necklace with ____'s teeth.
4.	CANOE	Mafatu built one for his trip home.
5.	COCONUT	Mafatu used its leaves to build a lean-to and drank its juice.
6.	CORAL	It forms the reefs.
7.	COURAGE	Polynesians worshipped it.
8.	DRUMS	The sound of these wakes Mafatu.
9.	EATERS	___-of-men chased Mafatu.
10.	FIFTEEN	Mafatu's age when he went off by himself
11.	FIRE	This at the base of the tree trunk helped Mafatu fell the tree for his canoe.
12.	FISHING	Occupation of the villagers
13.	FORBIDDEN	Where Mafatu landed & eaters-of-men made sacrifices: ___ Island
14.	FOUR	Number of eaters-of-men who chased Mafatu on the island
15.	GHOST	Tupapau or ___ spirit
16.	HEART	Mafatu's christened name: Stout ___
17.	HIKUERU	Island of Mafatu's home
18.	HURRICANE	Killed Mafatu's mother
19.	KANA	Youth who was friendly to Mafatu
20.	KIVI	Deformed albatross & Mafatu's companion
21.	KNIFE	Mafatu made this from whale bone
22.	LAND	Mafatu made new clothing to show he had conquered the ___.
23.	LIME	Mafatu treats his wound with ___ juice.
24.	MAFATU	The Boy Who Was Afraid
25.	MAUI	God of the Fishermen
26.	MOANA	The Sea God
27.	MULBERRY	This tree's bark lining was used to make clothing.
28.	PAREU	Clothing
29.	POLYNESIANS	Native people who lived on the islands
30.	RAFT	Mafatu built one so he could set fish traps.
31.	RUAU	Grandfather who told about the Smoking Islands
32.	SEA	Mafatu feared this.
33.	SHARK	Mafatu killed it by slitting its belly open with his knife.
34.	SMOKING	Home of the eaters-of-men: ___ Island
35.	SPEARHEAD	Mafatu stole it from the statue.
36.	STREAM	Mafatu collapses near one when he arrives at the island.
37.	TAHITI	Island where Mafatu thought he would arrive
38.	TAMANU	Tree used to make the canoe
39.	TAVANA	Chief; Mafatu's father: ___ Nui
40.	TEKOTO	Uninhabited islet where Mafatu and his mother landed
41.	THREE	Mafatu's age when his mother died
42.	URI	Canine companion to Mafatu
43.	WHALE	This skeleton was used for making tools.
44.	YELLOW	Color of Mafatu's dog

VOCABULARY RESOURCE MATERIALS

CALL IT COURAGE VOCABULARY WORD SEARCH

```
T A N T A L I Z I N G L U M I N O U S P E W F S
T S I P H O N E D M V L S F W H B S L G T B T R
D D K I G Z Q Z V J G V S M R H B U A Y J O E S
S F J M S C C I N Q M S J U F V K T D R Y L B X
R N D P N W H R S W Z C M T G R N E G M I S T Q
Q U H O M C F E V C K O J T Q A Y P J S J T A Y
L L D T S W A T T Y O R P E V L P M H L D E U K
I R R E S O L U T E C N E R E F F I D N I R T M
J B I N Q S O A T A K O G V G R N H N T S V S L
D Z N T N T E C P I G I I E Z G E S J N M D I T
E Z O L S L F S V N O S X Y A S U D Q C A E Q D
S V I V I B I E I F L N H S A L W N U I L C M V
I L T C D Z R H L U G E C Y T A E L A M O R L C
O U A L E I S Y V L R H H R N V P D I P P E P E
P R L D T I H N F G O E Y E O R A W L E P I R G
G E E A N Z O L N N T R D S I E D S I N R F O L
T D B I P C B I C I E P W T T Z M N D E L F X
S L M J D E R J B D S P R R R N E Q G I S S A C
E I W E J I R C W N Q A O A E I R W Y N S D N M
D S X H A K L I N E U P U P X Y C L B G I K E N
Q A B P V P P J L R E N G M E Z I G G V V K D D
W M S T U M U L T L D N H A X R Y P Q Y E H Y
S E I R A N O I S S I M T R A P R O S T R A T E
D D I S M A Y X T J C D W W I N E V I T A B L E
```

ADZE	DISMAY	INTERVALS	POISED	SULTRY
APPREHENSION	ELATION	IRRESOLUTE	PROFANED	TANTALIZING
BOLSTER	EXERTION	JEERED	PROSTRATE	TAUT
CAPSIZED	FELL	LASH	QUAILING	TUMULT
CAUTERIZE	FIERCE	LIVID	RAMPARTS	VANTAGE
CAUTION	GRACILE	LUMINOUS	RELISHING	VERITABLE
CONGEALED	GROTESQUE	LURED	RENDING	WANED
CONVULSIVELY	IMPENDING	MISSIONARIES	RUDE	WARILY
CULPRIT	IMPETUS	MUTTER	SCORN	WAXED
DESPAIRING	IMPOTENT	OPPRESSIVE	SEIZE	WROUGHT
DIMINISHING	INDIFFERENCE	PERIL	SIPHONED	
DISMAL	INEVITABLE	PINNACLE	STOUT	

CALL IT COURAGE VOCABULARY WORD SEARCH ANSWER KEY

ADZE	DISMAY	INTERVALS	POISED	SULTRY
APPREHENSION	ELATION	IRRESOLUTE	PROFANED	TANTALIZING
BOLSTER	EXERTION	JEERED	PROSTRATE	TAUT
CAPSIZED	FELL	LASH	QUAILING	TUMULT
CAUTERIZE	FIERCE	LIVID	RAMPARTS	VANTAGE
CAUTION	GRACILE	LUMINOUS	RELISHING	VERITABLE
CONGEALED	GROTESQUE	LURED	RENDING	WANED
CONVULSIVELY	IMPENDING	MISSIONARIES	RUDE	WARILY
CULPRIT	IMPETUS	MUTTER	SCORN	WAXED
DESPAIRING	IMPOTENT	OPPRESSIVE	SEIZE	WROUGHT
DIMINISHING	INDIFFERENCE	PERIL	SIPHONED	
DISMAL	INEVITABLE	PINNACLE	STOUT	

CALL IT COURAGE VOCABULARY CROSSWORD

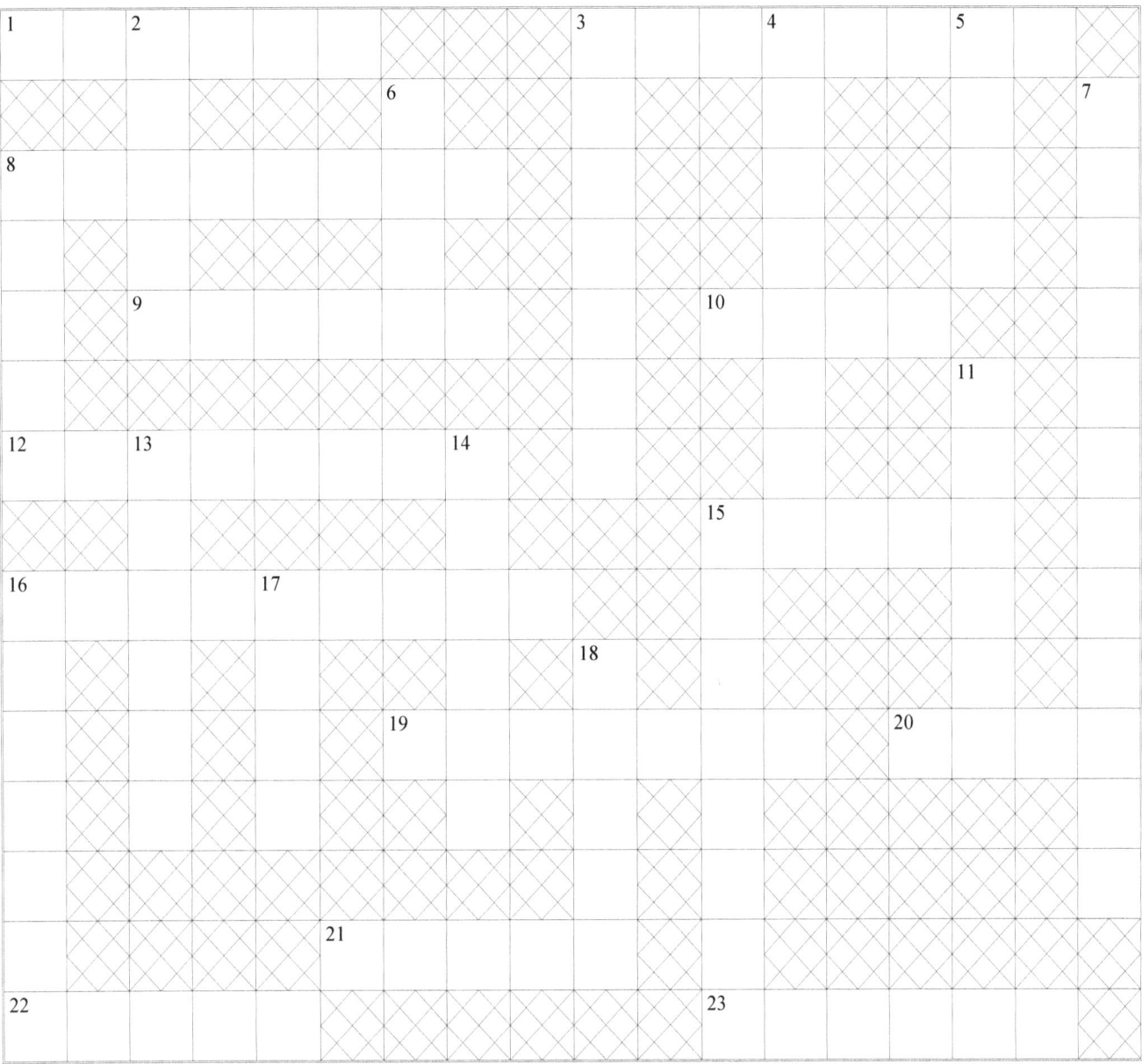

Across
1. Feeling of hopelessness or disappointment
3. Walls of a fort
8. Showed disrespect for gods or a religion
9. Noisy uproar
10. Tie something to another object
12. Giving off or reflecting light
15. Take hold of quickly and firmly
16. Distances between things
19. Formed; created
20. Tool for cutting heavy pieces of wood
21. Very angry
22. Contempt; disrespect
23. Depressing

Down
2. Brave; sturdy
3. Tearing apart violently
4. Top; highest point
5. Stiff; stretched tight
6. Cut down
7. In a violently jerking or shaking manner
8. Danger
11. Mocked by shouting or laughing
13. Complain quietly or indistinctly
14. Very hot and damp
15. Transferred liquid through a tube
16. Forward motion; movement
17. Rough; incomplete
18. Tempted someone to go somewhere

CALL IT COURAGE VOCABULARY CROSSWORD ANSWER KEY

	1 D	2 I	S	M	A	Y		3 R	4 A	M	P	5 A	R	T	S	
		T				6 F		E			I		A			7 C
8 P	R	O	F	A	N	E	D				N		U			O
E		U				L		D			N		T			N
R		9 T	U	M	U	L	T		I		10 L	A	S	H		V
I									N		C			11 J		U
12 L	U	13 M	I	N	O	14 U	S		G		L			E		L
		U				S					15 S	E	I	Z	E	S
16 I	N	17 T	E	R	V	A	L	S			I			R		I
M		T		U		T		18 L			P			E		V
P		E		19 D	W	R	O	U	G	H	T		20 A	D	Z	E
E		R		E		Y		R			O			L	
T								E			N					Y
U				21 L	I	V	I	D			E					
22 S	C	O	R	N							23 D	I	S	M	A	L

Across
1. Feeling of hopelessness or disappointment
3. Walls of a fort
8. Showed disrespect for gods or a religion
9. Noisy uproar
10. Tie something to another object
12. Giving off or reflecting light
15. Take hold of quickly and firmly
16. Distances between things
19. Formed; created
20. Tool for cutting heavy pieces of wood
21. Very angry
22. Contempt; disrespect
23. Depressing

Down
2. Brave; sturdy
3. Tearing apart violently
4. Top; highest point
5. Stiff; stretched tight
6. Cut down
7. In a violently jerking or shaking manner
8. Danger
11. Mocked by shouting or laughing
13. Complain quietly or indistinctly
14. Very hot and damp
15. Transferred liquid through a tube
16. Forward motion; movement
17. Rough; incomplete
18. Tempted someone to go somewhere

CALL IT COURAGE VOCABULARY MATCHING 1

___ 1. ADZE   A. Feeling of hopelessness or disappointment
___ 2. WANED   B. Ferocious; violent
___ 3. VANTAGE   C. Tool for cutting heavy pieces of wood
___ 4. PINNACLE   D. Impossible to prevent from happening
___ 5. CONVULSIVELY   E. Giving off or reflecting light
___ 6. CAUTION   F. Care; close attention
___ 7. SULTRY   G. Tie something to another object
___ 8. MISSIONARIES   H. Balanced; suspended
___ 9. VERITABLE   I. Brave; sturdy
___10. POISED   J. Real; true
___11. CAPSIZED   K. Very angry
___12. GROTESQUE   L. Top; highest point
___13. TANTALIZING   M. Position that gives an advantage
___14. LIVID   N. People sent by a church to spread its faith
___15. RENDING   O. Overturned; caused a boat to overturn
___16. WARILY   P. Showed disrespect for gods or a religion
___17. INEVITABLE   Q. Tempting but unavailable
___18. STOUT   R. Tearing apart violently
___19. LUMINOUS   S. Decreased; got smaller
___20. SEIZE   T. In a violently jerking or shaking manner
___21. PROFANED   U. Take hold of quickly and firmly
___22. DISMAY   V. Bizarre; gross
___23. LURED   W. Tempted someone to go somewhere
___24. LASH   X. Cautiously
___25. FIERCE   Y. Very hot and damp

CALL IT COURAGE VOCABULARY MATCHING 1 ANSWER KEY

C - 1. ADZE — A. Feeling of hopelessness or disappointment
S - 2. WANED — B. Ferocious; violent
M - 3. VANTAGE — C. Tool for cutting heavy pieces of wood
L - 4. PINNACLE — D. Impossible to prevent from happening
T - 5. CONVULSIVELY — E. Giving off or reflecting light
F - 6. CAUTION — F. Care; close attention
Y - 7. SULTRY — G. Tie something to another object
N - 8. MISSIONARIES — H. Balanced; suspended
J - 9. VERITABLE — I. Brave; sturdy
H - 10. POISED — J. Real; true
O - 11. CAPSIZED — K. Very angry
V - 12. GROTESQUE — L. Top; highest point
Q - 13. TANTALIZING — M. Position that gives an advantage
K - 14. LIVID — N. People sent by a church to spread its faith
R - 15. RENDING — O. Overturned; caused a boat to overturn
X - 16. WARILY — P. Showed disrespect for gods or a religion
D - 17. INEVITABLE — Q. Tempting but unavailable
I - 18. STOUT — R. Tearing apart violently
E - 19. LUMINOUS — S. Decreased; got smaller
U - 20. SEIZE — T. In a violently jerking or shaking manner
P - 21. PROFANED — U. Take hold of quickly and firmly
A - 22. DISMAY — V. Bizarre; gross
W - 23. LURED — W. Tempted someone to go somewhere
G - 24. LASH — X. Cautiously
B - 25. FIERCE — Y. Very hot and damp

CALL IT COURAGE VOCABULARY MATCHING 2

___ 1. RAMPARTS   A. Harsh
___ 2. DISMAL   B. Worry; nervousness
___ 3. PROSTRATE   C. Top; highest point
___ 4. TUMULT   D. Noisy uproar
___ 5. OPPRESSIVE   E. Bizarre; gross
___ 6. CAUTERIZE   F. Taking great pleasure in
___ 7. CAUTION   G. Seal a wound with something that burns
___ 8. QUAILING   H. Tearing apart violently
___ 9. TANTALIZING   I. Walls of a fort
___ 10. VERITABLE   J. Danger
___ 11. BOLSTER   K. Real; true
___ 12. SULTRY   L. Tempted someone to go somewhere
___ 13. LURED   M. Becoming smaller
___ 14. APPREHENSION   N. Tie something to another object
___ 15. POISED   O. Care; close attention
___ 16. LASH   P. Tempting but unavailable
___ 17. RELISHING   Q. Position that gives an advantage
___ 18. RENDING   R. Lie flat
___ 19. PINNACLE   S. Formed; created
___ 20. VANTAGE   T. Trembling or shrinking back with fear
___ 21. INDIFFERENCE   U. Balanced; suspended
___ 22. GROTESQUE   V. Depressing
___ 23. WROUGHT   W. Strengthen by encouraging
___ 24. PERIL   X. Very hot and damp
___ 25. DIMINISHING   Y. Lack of interest or concern

CALL IT COURAGE VOCABULARY MATCHING 2 ANSWER KEY

I - 1. RAMPARTS		A. Harsh
V - 2. DISMAL		B. Worry; nervousness
R - 3. PROSTRATE		C. Top; highest point
D - 4. TUMULT		D. Noisy uproar
A - 5. OPPRESSIVE		E. Bizarre; gross
G - 6. CAUTERIZE		F. Taking great pleasure in
O - 7. CAUTION		G. Seal a wound with something that burns
T - 8. QUAILING		H. Tearing apart violently
P - 9. TANTALIZING		I. Walls of a fort
K -10. VERITABLE		J. Danger
W 11. BOLSTER		K. Real; true
X -12. SULTRY		L. Tempted someone to go somewhere
L -13. LURED		M. Becoming smaller
B -14. APPREHENSION		N. Tie something to another object
U -15. POISED		O. Care; close attention
N -16. LASH		P. Tempting but unavailable
F -17. RELISHING		Q. Position that gives an advantage
H -18. RENDING		R. Lie flat
C -19. PINNACLE		S. Formed; created
Q -20. VANTAGE		T. Trembling or shrinking back with fear
Y -21. INDIFFERENCE		U. Balanced; suspended
E -22. GROTESQUE		V. Depressing
S -23. WROUGHT		W. Strengthen by encouraging
J - 24. PERIL		X. Very hot and damp
M 25. DIMINISHING		Y. Lack of interest or concern

CALL IT COURAGE VOCABULARY JUGGLE REVIEW 1

1. SAHL = 1. _____
Tie something to another object

2. EOSIDP = 2. _____
Balanced; suspended

3. UWHOGRT = 3. _____
Formed; created

4. BEEALVTRI = 4. _____
Real; true

5. IVLDI = 5. _____
Very angry

6. GIINNPDEM = 6. _____
About to happen

7. LLFE = 7. _____
Cut down

8. USMULION = 8. _____
Giving off or reflecting light

9. FDAPEONR = 9. _____
Showed disrespect for gods or a religion

10. NCEDALOGE =10. _____
Became thick or solid

11. DEULR =11. _____
Tempted someone to go somewhere

12. EARIOPNNSPHE =12. _____
Worry; nervousness

13. YWALIR =13. _____
Cautiously

14. IADSZPEC =14. _____
Overturned; caused a boat to overturn

15. EPTTMNIO =15. _____
Without strength

16. NATRSIVLE =16. _____
Distances between things

17. UDER =17. _____
Rough; incomplete

18. SLEBROT =18. _____
Strengthen by encouraging

19. ENVAGAT =19. _____
Position that gives an advantage

20. EBILTAENIV =20. _____
Impossible to prevent from happening

21. NSRCO =21. _____
Contempt; disrespect

22. TQSEUGROE =22. _____
Bizarre; gross

23. ANTOICU =23. _____
Care; close attention

24. SPORATERT =24. _____
Lie flat

25. RSPTAAMR =25. _____
Walls of a fort

26. RSIPOEEVSP =26. _____
Harsh

27. AEDZ =27. _____
Tool for cutting heavy pieces of wood

28. NTXREEOI =28. _____
Physical effort

29. GNIRDEN =29. _____
Tearing apart violently

CALL IT COURAGE VOCABULARY JUGGLE REVIEW 1 ANSWER KEY

1. SAHL = 1. LASH
   Tie something to another object

2. EOSIDP = 2. POISED
   Balanced; suspended

3. UWHOGRT = 3. WROUGHT
   Formed; created

4. BEEALVTRI = 4. VERITABLE
   Real; true

5. IVLDI = 5. LIVID
   Very angry

6. GIINNPDEM = 6. IMPENDING
   About to happen

7. LLFE = 7. FELL
   Cut down

8. USMULION = 8. LUMINOUS
   Giving off or reflecting light

9. FDAPEONR = 9. PROFANED
   Showed disrespect for gods or a religion

10. NCEDALOGE = 10. CONGEALED
    Became thick or solid

11. DEULR = 11. LURED
    Tempted someone to go somewhere

12. EARIOPNNSPHE = 12. APPREHENSION
    Worry; nervousness

13. YWALIR = 13. WARILY
    Cautiously

14. IADSZPEC = 14. CAPSIZED
    Overturned; caused a boat to overturn

15. EPTTMNIO = 15. IMPOTENT
    Without strength

16. NATRSIVLE	=16.	INTERVALS
		Distances between things
17. UDER	=17.	RUDE
		Rough; incomplete
18. SLEBROT	=18.	BOLSTER
		Strengthen by encouraging
19. ENVAGAT	=19.	VANTAGE
		Position that gives an advantage
20. EBILTAENIV	=20.	INEVITABLE
		Impossible to prevent from happening
21. NSRCO	=21.	SCORN
		Contempt; disrespect
22. TQSEUGROE	=22.	GROTESQUE
		Bizarre; gross
23. ANTOICU	=23.	CAUTION
		Care; close attention
24. SPORATERT	=24.	PROSTRATE
		Lie flat
25. RSPTAAMR	=25.	RAMPARTS
		Walls of a fort
26. RSIPOEEVSP	=26.	OPPRESSIVE
		Harsh
27. AEDZ	=27.	ADZE
		Tool for cutting heavy pieces of wood
28. NTXREEOI	=28.	EXERTION
		Physical effort
29. GNIRDEN	=29.	RENDING
		Tearing apart violently

CALL IT COURAGE JUGGLE LETTER REVIEW 2

1. RDEEJE = 1. _____
   Mocked by shouting or laughing

2. GREADSNIIP = 2. _____
   Feeling hopeless

3. ETUZACEIR = 3. _____
   Seal a wound with something that burns

4. TMREUT = 4. _____
   Complain quietly or indistinctly

5. UTMTLU = 5. _____
   Noisy uproar

6. LIRUCTP = 6. _____
   Someone who is responsible for a misdeed

7. EZIES = 7. _____
   Take hold of quickly and firmly

8. INTEOAL = 8. _____
   Feeling of extraordinary happiness and excitement

9. IGAANZTTNIL = 9. _____
   Tempting but unavailable

10. AYIDSM =10. _____
    Feeling of hopelessness or disappointment

11. EFNRFIENIDCE =11. _____
    Lack of interest or concern

12. ANCEPNIL =12. _____
    Top; highest point

13. NIOSPHDE =13. _____
    Transferred liquid through a tube

14. ESRNIHGLI =14. _____
    Taking great pleasure in

15. TAUT =15. _____
    Stiff; stretched tight

16. WEDXA =16. _____
Increased; enlarged

17. YUTSRL =17. _____
Very hot and damp

18. IDAMSL =18. _____
Depressing

19. ISENORAISSMI =19. _____
People sent by a church to spread its faith

20. IELPR =20. _____
Danger

21. IEFCER =21. _____
Ferocious; violent

22. SHNIDIIGMNI =22. _____
Becoming smaller

23. LCRIEAG =23. _____
Gracefully slender

24. TOUTS =24. _____
Brave; sturdy

25. PEITMSU =25. _____
Forward motion; movement

26. LVONUYISVLEC =26. _____
In a violently jerking or shaking manner

27. IGANILQU =27. _____
Trembling or shrinking back with fear

28. LITORRUEES =28. _____
Unsure; not able to make decisions

29. ANWED =29. _____
Decreased; got smaller

CALL IT COURAGE JUGGLE REVIEW 2 ANSWER KEY

1. RDEEJE = 1. JEERED
   Mocked by shouting or laughing

2. GREADSNIIP = 2. DESPAIRING
   Feeling hopeless

3. ETUZACEIR = 3. CAUTERIZE
   Seal a wound with something that burns

4. TMREUT = 4. MUTTER
   Complain quietly or indistinctly

5. UTMTLU = 5. TUMULT
   Noisy uproar

6. LIRUCTP = 6. CULPRIT
   Someone who is responsible for a misdeed

7. EZIES = 7. SEIZE
   Take hold of quickly and firmly

8. INTEOAL = 8. ELATION
   Feeling of extraordinary happiness and excitement

9. IGAANZTTNIL = 9. TANTALIZING
   Tempting but unavailable

10. AYIDSM =10. DISMAY
    Feeling of hopelessness or disappointment

11. EFNRFIENIDCE =11. INDIFFERENCE
    Lack of interest or concern

12. ANCEPNIL =12. PINNACLE
    Top; highest point

13. NIOSPHDE =13. SIPHONED
    Transferred liquid through a tube

14. ESRNIHGLI =14. RELISHING
    Taking great pleasure in

15. TAUT =15. TAUT
    Stiff; stretched tight

16. WEDXA	=16.	WAXED
		Increased; enlarged
17. YUTSRL	=17.	SULTRY
		Very hot and damp
18. IDAMSL	=18.	DISMAL
		Depressing
19. ISENORAISSMI	=19.	MISSIONARIES
		People sent by a church to spread its faith
20. IELPR	=20.	PERIL
		Danger
21. IEFCER	=21.	FIERCE
		Ferocious; violent
22. SHNIDIIGMNI	=22.	DIMINISHING
		Becoming smaller
23. LCRIEAG	=23.	GRACILE
		Gracefully slender
24. TOUTS	=24.	STOUT
		Brave; sturdy
25. PEITMSU	=25.	IMPETUS
		Forward motion; movement
26. LVONUYISVLEC	=26.	CONVULSIVELY
		In a violently jerking or shaking manner
27. IGANILQU	=27.	QUAILING
		Trembling or shrinking back with fear
28. LITORRUEES	=28.	IRRESOLUTE
		Unsure; not able to make decisions
29. ANWED	=29.	WANED
		Decreased; got smaller

Call It Courage Vocabulary Word List

No.	Word	Clue/Definition
1.	ADZE	Tool for cutting heavy pieces of wood
2.	APPREHENSION	Worry; nervousness
3.	BOLSTER	Strengthen by encouraging
4.	CAPSIZED	Overturned; caused a boat to overturn
5.	CAUTERIZE	Seal a wound with something that burns
6.	CAUTION	Care; close attention
7.	CONGEALED	Became thick or solid
8.	CONVULSIVELY	In a violently jerking or shaking manner
9.	CULPRIT	Someone who is responsible for a misdeed
10.	DESPAIRING	Feeling hopeless
11.	DIMINISHING	Becoming smaller
12.	DISMAL	Depressing
13.	DISMAY	Feeling of hopelessness or disappointment
14.	ELATION	Feeling of extraordinary happiness and excitement
15.	EXERTION	Physical effort
16.	FELL	Cut down
17.	FIERCE	Ferocious; violent
18.	GRACILE	Gracefully slender
19.	GROTESQUE	Bizarre; gross
20.	IMPENDING	About to happen
21.	IMPETUS	Forward motion; movement
22.	IMPOTENT	Without strength
23.	INDIFFERENCE	Lack of interest or concern
24.	INEVITABLE	Impossible to prevent from happening
25.	INTERVALS	Distances between things
26.	IRRESOLUTE	Unsure; not able to make decisions
27.	JEERED	Mocked by shouting or laughing
28.	LASH	Tie something to another object
29.	LIVID	Very angry
30.	LUMINOUS	Giving off or reflecting light
31.	LURED	Tempted someone to go somewhere
32.	MISSIONARIES	People sent by a church to spread its faith
33.	MUTTER	Complain quietly or indistinctly
34.	OPPRESSIVE	Harsh
35.	PERIL	Danger
36.	PINNACLE	Top; highest point
37.	POISED	Balanced; suspended
38.	PROFANED	Showed disrespect for gods or a religion
39.	PROSTRATE	Lie flat
40.	QUAILING	Trembling or shrinking back with fear
41.	RAMPARTS	Walls of a fort
42.	RELISHING	Taking great pleasure in
43.	RENDING	Tearing apart violently
44.	RUDE	Rough; incomplete
45.	SCORN	Contempt; disrespect
46.	SEIZE	Take hold of quickly and firmly
47.	SIPHONED	Transferred liquid through a tube
48.	STOUT	Brave; sturdy
49.	SULTRY	Very hot and damp
50.	TANTALIZING	Tempting but unavailable
51.	TAUT	Stiff; stretched tight

Call It Courage Vocabulary Word List Continued

No.	Word	Clue/Definition
52.	TUMULT	Noisy uproar
53.	VANTAGE	Position that gives an advantage
54.	VERITABLE	Real; true
55.	WANED	Decreased; got smaller
56.	WARILY	Cautiously
57.	WAXED	Increased; enlarged
58.	WROUGHT	Formed; created

www.ingramcontent.com/pod-product-compliance
Lightning Source LLC
Chambersburg PA
CBHW051409070526
44584CB00023B/3356